Spiritual DNA

William J. Brannan

PRESS

—〰—

To my family both natural and spiritual and to Jesus who is head of all.

Table of Contents

—ɱ—

As Iron Sharpens Iron

—w—

I am a firm believer in church. Because I am committed to Jesus I have no choice but to be committed to church. What I mean when I say that I am committed to church is that I am committed to what I understand to be the biblical pattern for church. It must bear the fruit of biblical church, and that is a manifestation of the kingdom of God in the midst of men, and the life of Christ being fully reproduced. I believe we all need to ask ourselves whether we believe that what we are committed to is actually able to fulfill the mandate of church. If not we either need to reform it or get out. We must not identify with a church simply because we like it or we are comfortable there. We must believe that what we are committed to has the potential to fulfill the Biblical mandate for church.

One of the saddest things I have seen is people who are involved with a ministry because it validates them as a person or as a Christian. People are often invested in a ministry because of how it makes them feel and not because they really believe in it. If I have a goal to cross the ocean, I would not want to build an automobile. I might invest much time and money and build a wonderful automobile, but it will not get me across the ocean. That is what many Christians are doing today, they are invested in ministries that, even if they are fully successful at what they do, are not able to fulfill the mandate of Church. Every Christian has the exact same responsibility to fulfill the great commission, and the only biblical way to do that is to be committed to a church that is able to accomplish it.

When I was a senior in high school I did a musical at the church I had grown up in. I hadn't been to church for years because I never experienced God there. Although I went to be part of the musical, I was also spying on the church. I wanted to see if God was there. I discovered that the youth of the church were drinking, doing drugs and sleeping around, and basically I didn't see any difference between the church and the world. I concluded it wasn't for me.

My conversion to Christianity happened about a year later when I had a very powerful encounter with God that I was not looking for. I had an encounter with spiritual reality during my conversion where I saw that if people were not in Christ then they were dead in sin. I knew that the most important thing in the world is that every person be reconciled to God. At one point during my conversion I started praising God and declaring, "Lord, this is not what they taught me in church. You are not a God who is far away. You are here!" I was converted to a religion where God is real today, not only yesterday or tomorrow.

I came to know Him and fellowship with Him as normal life—not abnormal life. The Holy Spirit is a wonderful companion and teacher. He showed me that many things were sinful long before I ever knew in the scriptures how to prove it. I knew it simply because the presence of God would be broken. Fellowship with the Holy Spirit is invigorating and transformational. For example, I read through the Bible like a maniac because God seemed to leap off of the pages into my consciousness. I didn't read through the Bible because this would make me look spiritual, it was spiritual, an encounter with the living God. This is why we need to build church in such a way that people come into a real relationship with God and not into a form of religion that pleases men. We need to develop people to have a real relationship with God for themselves and not to live to try to please the people of the church. They must learn to please the Lord.

After my conversion there were many people that I could have brought to church, but the problem was that I couldn't find anywhere that I knew that they would encounter God and be knit into a body where they could grow up in Him. The closest church that I could find to Biblical church, is not considered a church at all. It was the Word of God community in Ann Arbor, Michigan. There were people there who knew the Lord and the Holy Spirit in a way that was much deeper than most churches that were around.

That community was a great blessing to me as a new Christian. There was a small bible study for youth that met every two weeks on a Friday night.

They asked me to run it. God in His grace grew it into a college, high school and middle school ministry that was planting clubs at local schools. Yet it wasn't the size or the outward success that made it really special. It became a place where people met God! People were continually being born again and filled with the Holy Spirit. It was wonderful.

People met God in many wonderful ways. We would often have people who were not Christians who would gather outside where we met. One night someone asked me to speak with two young men who had been curiously gathered outside for several weeks. We were sitting in an office and talking about things that had nothing to do with the kingdom of God. Suddenly one of the young men stood up and declared that he would never serve a God who condemns people simply because they don't believe in Jesus. We never told him that, and besides that isn't exactly how we believe it. He doesn't condemn them because they don't believe. They are already condemned because of sin, and believing in Jesus is the only way to be un-condemned. People are already spiritually dead, and the gospel is an invitation to come to life. Immediately these two young men stormed out of there and drove off. The very next week they came and asked to speak with me. They told me that immediately after leaving, while they were driving off, they encountered the Holy Spirit and they gave their lives to Jesus! Such stories and experiences were common.

I remember a football player at a local high school who decided he would come to one of the small groups. He was going to follow some people who were going there from school in his car. Immediately a group of people came over and began ridiculing him and telling him that he really shouldn't go. He went to the group anyway. Afterwards I was curious what he thought, so I asked him. He told me that it was the first time in his life that he didn't have to wear a mask. He said it was the first time he felt free to be himself. He experienced Christian love and freedom from the fear of men. He experienced the kingdom of God at that small group!

There is an alternative high school in downtown Ann Arbor. I knew a girl who went there, and from her perspective there was no one at that time who went there that didn't smoke marijuana and drink. There were three people professing to believe in Jesus and she was one. I met one of the other ones, and she told me her mom was a pastor and that she had been to three weddings recently and they were all homosexual. Even the professing Christians acknowledged that they didn't actually know the Lord. That school caused a very anti-authority attitude in the people. I remember a teacher from Washtenaw Community College who told me that she can usually tell the very first week of class who came from Community High. She could tell because whenever she assigned work they would challenge her and ask why they should have to do the work. The people from that school were involved in all kinds of religion, humanistic philosophy and were very intellectually proud. My friend John Luton and I went down there and tried to talk with them. We always started with chit chat. Every time we could sense the conversation was going to shift to the spiritual, something would happen to take the students away. John looked at me and said, "there are evil spirits at work here." So we prayed a simple little prayer "Lord, give us more angels than they have demons." I know it sounds silly but it worked. Within half an hour we were sitting out front with a group of people talking about Jesus. We went there once a week and chatted with students who would gather. One week a guy was arguing for all he was worth about being an atheist. The next week they brought out their "Goliath", a guy who was very intellectual and was involved actively in the occult. Eventually I challenged him and asked him to let me pray for him. I told him that I would pray for him and God would reveal Himself to him. At first he profusely refused. I told him that he was refusing because he knew I was telling the truth and He didn't want to have to face it. Finally he let me pray for him. Immediately after I was done praying for him, that young man who had argued with me the week before spoke up. I believe that he actually prophesied. He looked that other man straight in the face, pointed his finger at him and declared "Now when Jesus reveals himself to you, do not deny it." Later, I said to him, "I thought you were an atheist." "Not anymore," he replied.

I could go on telling stories about the wonderful things that God was doing there. Authentic spiritual life permeated the whole work. People boldly testified of the glory and power of knowing Jesus, because they actually lived in spiritual fellowship with God and one another. That is Christian unity.

As time went on, I began to outgrow what I was doing at the Word of God. There were certain restrictions that would keep the work limited to a certain sphere of activity. There was real spiritual life that was growing, but it needed structures that would allow it to come to maturity. Although in one sense it was authentic church, in another sense, it could never be authentic church because it would eventually come to a place where it could grow no further. Not only that, the life we were experiencing would often be a crutch for people who were part of churches that were lacking spiritual life. The bottom line is that although we would be able to bring people into a real encounter with the life of Jesus, because we couldn't acknowledge that what we were was a baby church we could never nurture that life to maturity. Eventually people would have to move on and many would end up in churches that restrict spiritual growth. That is very irresponsible. It would be like having a baby who, when they turn four, you drop them off in the middle of New York to fend for themselves. We have a responsibility to build churches where people of all generations, cultures, and social status are able to grow to maturity and are able to fulfill the ministry God has appointed for them. Anything less than this is using people to perpetuate something that falls short of the biblical mandate to make disciples.

I remember talking with someone who was both a leader in one of the local churches and in the Sword of the Spirit community. (That is the other half of the Word of God church split.) I told this man that as a leader of his church he had a responsibility to build community life in his church. He told me that is not what church is for. He told me that church is where you get your doctrine and sacraments and the community is where you get fellowship and life in the spirit. That is absolute nonsense to me. I told him that for the vast majority of people in his church, that church was the only Christian life that they know and it has to be complete.

I believe that every church should have the type life that God originally invested in the Word of God community and that it should be structured to nurture that life to maturity. It wasn't just the Word of God community where God invested that life; it is the very same spiritual life that is found wherever people come into fellowship with God and one another. From the time that I came to know the community I tried to investigate why the people there had a much richer experience of coming to and knowing Jesus than many other churches. I discovered it was because they were a group of people who had unity around a living encounter with Jesus. It was alive and real. That unity translated into a mission to bring all people into a real relationship with the Holy Spirit. No wonder it had real spiritual momentum.

I remember being enamored by the testimonies of people in the community. Many had conversion experiences as wild as mine. They had encounters with the Spirit of God just like I had. They experienced the gifts of the spirit in many ways. From the very beginning I experienced God working in wonderful ways there. Yet the model of church is that they are an ecumenical community where everyone is meant to belong to another church. In practice it was actually a supplemental or secondary church. Whenever it had spiritual momentum it became the place where people got their primary teaching and fellowship, and where they gave their primary investment. I do not see how this is anything less than church with restrictions.

What I would suggest is that the people experienced something of Christianity that is meant to be in all churches. It was this vision that the life that I experienced in the Word of God community is absolutely foundational to church that caused me to move on from there. I had to make a choice. I could continue where I was already comfortable, had a good reputation, and had natural stability, but the cost would be knowing that it was at the expense of what I believed in. The other option is that I could start over again. As it turned out, I came to be involved with King's Way Connection. The very same movement of the Spirit that brought forth expressions such as ecumenical communities also went a separate direction with others which was to develop networks of churches around a common experience of the kingdom of God.

It is this common life of a people that is the context where we can grow to maturity. One of the sad realities that I have noticed is that many people go to church for their whole lives and never get set free from the sins that rob them of life. Much of this is due to lack of fellowship with people who are full of faith and the Holy Spirit. We become like those we have fellowship with. If we have fellowship with people who have a living fellowship with God and one another we will find it transformational. I am not talking about some mystical thing here, I am talking about simply growing in love. We need the messiness of community, where, we love one another even in the midst of offenses and failures for us to be secure enough to grow up. We must be committed to the family of God in a way where if we get offended we do not simply walk away. We have to be committed because we believe in it and not simply because of how it makes us feel.

Marriage is a wonderful example: it creates families. When a couple is married, when they have made that unbreakable covenant to one another for better or for worse, it provides a context where people are free to grow because they know they will not be forsaken. (This is assuming it is a healthy marriage built not just on feelings but also on covenantal commitment and Biblical love.) Marriage is the only context where romantic love becomes mature love. Romantic love is beautiful, mature love is glorious. The covenant of marriage creates a context for growth. For example, couples are free to have conflict because their covenant and love will cause even the conflicts to turn around for growth. The same pattern is true in the church. It is that deep commitment to God and one another that provides a context where we are free to grow. The potential for growth is no less than to be conformed into the image of Christ. Just so people understand, this is the very opposite of cookie cutter Christianity. Instead of restricting people into a mold that is devoid of diversity, it actually releases the infinite beauty of Christ to be manifested in His people. In that infinite diversity it also has many things that are allowed and things that are not allowed. For example, boredom, depression, self-righteousness, pride, and darkness of any kind you will not find in Jesus, and eventually you will not find it in people when they are fully conformed into His image. I can't wait. Love, mercy, grace, joy, peace and light of every kind is in Jesus and will be manifested in all who are conformed to His image. We will not all look the same but we will all look glorious. A river, an ocean, a sunset, a tree, an animal, a star, and all kinds of things are beautiful and glorious, yet they are not all exactly alike. This is how we will be in Christ.

We must build communities or rather churches where people reach their full potential in Christ, where we have fellowship that causes us all to grow in Christ.

"As iron sharpens iron, So a man sharpens the countenance of his friend." (Pr 27:17 NKJV)

This little verse is a very good description of biblical church. I want my countenance sharpened. How? Through my friends who invest life in me rather than death. We can look at David for some instruction.

David was a man who you could argue was full of faith and the Holy Spirit. He had a real relationship with God. He was of a different spirit than that of the established system, even from that of his brothers.

When the whole army of God was cowering before the Philistines because of Goliath, David, a little shepherd boy stands up because his spirit cannot believe that any army of man can oppose that which is of God, and so he slays Goliath. He put his trust in God and not his human combat training, his superior size and strength, or the numbers of his army. His trust was in the Lord and God honored that faith. That faith caused David to lead Saul's armies into great victories. He was of a different spirit.

There was one person who took notice of David from the beginning, because he also was of a different spirit. That was Jonathan, Saul's son. He was also a man full of faith and the Holy Spirit. One time when Israel was fighting the Philistines Jonathan took his armor-bearer to fight a whole garrison of 600 Philistines by themselves.

> "Then Jonathan said to the young man who bore his armor, "Come, let us go over to the garrison of these uncircumcised; it may be that the Lord will work for us. For nothing restrains the Lord from saving by many or by few."" (1 Sa 14:6 NKJV)

Such a beautiful spirit. No wonder he and David became great friends. They had unity of the spirit. All those who cowered at the challenges of Goliath also had unity—but of a different spirit. These two stood out in their generation. Listen to how Jonathan responds to hearing the report of David from Abner, the commander of Saul's army informing the king of who the boy was that slew Goliath.

> "Now when he had finished speaking to Saul, the soul of Jonathan was knit to the soul of David, and Jonathan loved him as his own soul. Saul took him that day, and would not let him go home to his father's house anymore. Then Jonathan and David made a covenant, because he loved him as his own soul. And Jonathan took off the robe that was on him and gave it to David, with his armor, even to his sword and his bow and his belt." (1 Sa 18:1-4 NKJV)

Jonathan saw the spirit that was in David and he loved him. He loved him because it was the exact same spirit of the Lord whom he loved. They had unity in the spirit and the bond of that love is very strong. He loved the very same spirit that provoked his father Saul to jealousy. It caused Saul to desire to kill David. Look how Jonathan sharpened the countenance of his friend when the Holy Spirit in David put his life in jeopardy.

> "So David saw that Saul had come out to seek his life. And David was in the Wilderness of Ziph in a forest. Then Jonathan, Saul's son, arose and went to David in the woods and strengthened his hand in God. And he said to him, "Do not fear, for the hand of Saul my father shall not find you. You shall be king

over Israel, and I shall be next to you. Even my father Saul knows that." So the two of them made a covenant before the Lord. And David stayed in the woods, and Jonathan went to his own house." (1 Sa 23:15-18 NKJV)

I think one of the saddest testimonies in all of scripture is that of Jonathan. Like those who did not heed the call to come out of Babylon, and when Babylon was destroyed, went down with it so Jonathan did not leave the house of Saul and identify with the house of David. He should have been with David in the wilderness where the Spirit of God in David matured him and reproduced in his house. Listen to David's response when he hears the news of the fall of the house of Saul. It is absolutely beautiful and shows the spirit that David was of. This mature love is a result of how David responded to his wilderness wanderings. There is no bitterness, no un-forgiveness; his heart was never against but always for Saul. Even when he had opportunities to kill Saul he wouldn't. He did not promote himself in the flesh but waited upon the Lord. Spiritual life grew in David and the love it produced covered a multitude of sin. His heart was for the glory of God and for the glory of God's people. He is ready to be king of Israel.

"Then David lamented with this lamentation over Saul and over Jonathan his son, and he told them to teach the children of Judah the Song of the Bow; indeed it is written in the

Book of Jasher: "The beauty of Israel is slain on your high places! How the mighty have fallen! Tell it not in Gath, Proclaim it not in the streets of Ashkelon— Lest the daughters of the Philistines rejoice, Lest the daughters of the uncircumcised triumph. "O mountains of Gilboa, Let there be no dew nor rain upon you, Nor fields of offerings. For the shield of the mighty is cast away there! The shield of Saul, not anointed with oil. From the blood of the slain, From the fat of the mighty, The bow of Jonathan did not turn back, And the sword of Saul did not return empty. "Saul and Jonathan were beloved and pleasant in their lives, And in their death they were not divided; They were swifter than eagles, They were stronger than lions. "O daughters of Israel, weep over Saul, Who clothed you in scarlet, with luxury; Who put ornaments of gold on your apparel. "How the mighty have fallen in the midst of the battle! Jonathan was slain in your high places. I am distressed for you, my brother Jonathan; You have been very pleasant to me; Your love to me was wonderful, Surpassing the love of women. "How the mighty have fallen, And the weapons of war perished!"" (2 Sa 1:17-27 NKJV)

Look at how wonderful a work God did in David in the wilderness. He had been full of faith and the Holy Spirit when he slew Goliath and led Saul's armies. Yet that was accomplished when David was in immaturity. Look at him now after maturing in the wilderness. Truly he is a man after God's own heart. His time of maturing in the wilderness brought forth a beautiful manifestation of the grace and love of God.

Yet there is something more. His spirit was contagious. Maturity is always fruitful; it has the power to reproduce itself. Take a look of how David's spirit reproduced a different spirit in his army than the spirit that was in Saul's. Saul trusted in his stature, his strength, his training, his politics, and his power. Where did that leave them? In fear before Goliath. How about David's army? Just look at a snap shot of the spirit of his army.

"These are the names of the mighty men whom David had: Josheb-Basshebeth the Tachmonite, chief among the captains. He was called Adino the Eznite, because he had killed eight hundred men at one time. And after him was Eleazar the son of Dodo, the Ahohite, one of the three mighty men with David when they defied the Philistines who were gathered there for battle, and the men of Israel had retreated. He arose and attacked the Philistines until his hand was weary, and his hand stuck to the sword. The Lord brought about a great victory that day; and the people returned after him only to plunder. And after him was Shammah the son of Agee the Hararite. The Philistines had gathered together into a troop where there was a piece of ground full of lentils. So the people fled from the Philistines. But he stationed himself in the middle of the field, defended it, and killed the Philistines. So the Lord brought about a great victory." (2 Sa 23:8-12 NKJV)

There is a natural growth that takes place when people are in fellowship with that which is in fellowship with God. It is transformational and it brings forth something wonderful, something unusual, something of a different spirit. This something is the life of Christ, it is what will prevail in the church before the end. Maybe right now the wages of those who serve this kingdom is a cave and tribulations, but there is going to be a changing of the order. It is already ordained in heaven and the time is coming when the house of Saul will lie in ruins. We need to clean our house so we do not go down with Babylon.

Let us look at the Corinthians for a moment. They thought that spiritually they were the stuff. They had the gifts of the Spirit; they are radical for Jesus. They praised louder, they preached longer, they danced harder than any church. You can imagine them saying, "Go ahead compare us to any other church and you will see that we are head and shoulders above the rest." There was only one problem. There was un-tolerable sin in the midst. A man was sleeping with his father's wife, his step-mother. Listen to the exhortation of Paul that followed his rebuke for this situation:

"Your glorying is not good. Do you not know that a little leaven leavens the whole lump? Therefore purge out the old leaven, that you may be a new lump, since you truly are unleavened. For indeed Christ, our Passover, was sacrificed for us. Therefore let us keep the feast, not with old leaven, nor with the leaven of malice and wickedness, but with the unleavened bread of sincerity and truth." (1 Co 5:6-8 NKJV)

We need to know what leaven is operating in our fellowship, and we need to allow the good and even invite in good leaven that we do not already have. The other side of this is that we need to get out the bad leaven. It is a disease that will infect the whole lump. We have to get it out and not compromise with it at all. It is deadly. It will lead us to a place where the enemies of God triumph over us. We need to get it out, and not allow any of it to get in. Paul is making it clear that this principle holds in every situation and not just the particular situation that the Corinthians were in.

"I wrote to you in my epistle not to keep company with sexually immoral people. Yet I certainly did not mean with the sexually immoral people of this world, or with the covetous, or extortioners, or idolaters, since then you would need to go out of the world. But now I have written to you not to keep company with anyone named a brother, who

Spiritual DNA

is sexually immoral, or covetous, or an idol-
ater, or a reviler, or a drunkard, or an extor-
tioner— not even to eat with such a person."
(1 Co 5:9-11 NKJV)

Look how bold is Paul's exhortation; do not even
eat with such people. Why? Because we become
like that which we have fellowship with. There is
a natural way in which we will have relationships
with people at work, at school, and in the normal
course of life who are bound in sin. Our love and
witness could be the very grace of God that brings
them to Christ. We are not to flee these situations
because of the sin, but rather to thrust out laborers
into such harvests. Yet, we will be worthless in our
endeavors to be the salt of the world if we are not
engaged in spiritual fellowship which is church. We
need a healthy fellowship to bring people to where
they will experience the transformational power of
God's love. If our fellowship is not fellowship with
the light but has let in the leaven of darkness, it is
good for nothing and will be destroyed by the Lord
Himself. Sin is no joke, and neither is dead religion.
We need to break our fellowship with everything that
is dead, and only have fellowship with that which is
alive. Such fellowship is transformational.

If we have fellowship with people like David,
we will become like David. If we have fellowship
with people who are like Paul, we will become like
Paul. The bottom line is that if we have fellowship
with people who are like Jesus, we will become like
Jesus. The beauty is that we will actually become like

Jesus by being in fellowship with other people who
have fellowship with Jesus. This is what church is all
about. This is the type of church we need to develop
and be very intentional about.

The beauty is that we can actually develop
church where people will come to spiritual maturity.
The pattern is given in scripture and there is no better
blueprint than the book of acts. Take a look.

"And they continued steadfastly in the apostles' doctrine and fellowship, in the breaking
of bread, and in prayers. Then fear came
upon every soul, and many wonders and
signs were done through the apostles. Now
all who believed were together, and had all
things in common, and sold their possessions
and goods, and divided them among all, as
anyone had need. So continuing daily with
one accord in the temple, and breaking bread
from house to house, they ate their food with
gladness and simplicity of heart, praising God
and having favor with all the people. And the
Lord added to the church daily those who
were being saved." (Ac 2:42-47 NKJV)

If we build with the Biblical pattern we will bear
the exact same fruit. There is no secret about it. The
exact same fruit will be the life of Christ reproduced
in us. We need to be very careful about the leaven.
The apostles' doctrine is doctrine that actually has
the power to conform people's lives to Christ. If
there are doctrines that restrict that life, we need to

get them out. Fellowship is with God and with people who are in fellowship with Him. If there is fellowship with darkness we need to get it out. Breaking of bread is the New Covenant renewal ceremony and it testifies of all that took place at the cross. If we are celebrating it in an old covenant way we need to get this leaven out. The cross is the foundation of everything, and if it is compromised or limited in any way we have a big problem. Prayer is the power generator that makes the whole thing a mighty force to be reckoned with. Prayerlessness needs to be eradicated. The early church held all things in common so no one lacked anything. Anything less than such a radical commitment needs to get out.

They continued daily in the temple and house to house. They were very intentional about church and made no excuses. Neither should we. Do you think that these people worked? Do you think they may have had busy lives? We always have time for what we value the most. The kingdom of God must be the pearl of great price that we sell all to possess. Any compromise of such a spirit in the church is bad leaven. Get it out. The biblical pattern of church removes all restrictions to the life of Christ and so God added to their numbers daily. Not weekly but daily. We can bear the same fruit. This church did everything to serve the life of Christ, and they did it no matter the cost. They made no excuses, so must we if we want to bear the same fruit. Many people would like the same fruit but they don't want to pay the same cost. I praise Jesus that we can bear the very same fruit. We need to develop churches where we are of one accord on this matter. I praise God, because such is the opportunity that is set before us.

It is all in the seed

—ɰ—

I remember the first time God called me to go to Africa. Before I left, the Lord gave me several teachings for the people. After I was prepared to go, I had a dream where I saw my good friend who had invited me to come. In the dream, as he heard what I was teaching he became uneasy, but as I opened up the scriptures concerning sonship he began to rejoice and praise the Lord. Then he said to me "Bill, if the people who had translated the scriptures had known this truth, the whole thing would have been over by now!" Granted, I find that hard to believe but it sure was an interesting and encouraging dream. I do not believe we make doctrines from dreams and visions, but they are often encouraging and help us to move forward with the Lord. Anyway, while I was staying at his house in Zambia, I figured I might as well ask the Lord to give me an example of a scripture that speaks concerning sonship where there is a pressure to conform its interpretation to fit with our preconceived doctrines. I find He usually waits to be asked. While I was praying I saw a vision of a scroll, and on it was written 1 John 3:9. I reached down and picked up the bible that was sitting on the table that happened to be a NIV version and it read:

"No one who is born of God will continue to sin, because God's seed remains in him; he cannot go on sinning, because he has been born of God." (1 Jn 3:9 NIV)

Now this was very interesting to me because I remember wrestling over this scripture when I had to translate it back in Greek class. I do not care what anyone tries to tell me, as far as I am concerned theology plays a significant role both in bible translation and interpretation whether we realize it or not. I remember wrestling with this passage in my studies because it seemed very difficult to reconcile with my experience. For example, another translation puts it in a way that is very hard to reconcile with most people's theology.

"Whoever has been born of God does not sin, for His seed remains in him; and he cannot sin, because he has been born of God." (1 Jn 3:9 NKJV)

The problem I had with this scripture was that I knew I was born again and also that I still sinned. If the Bible says that those who are born of God cannot sin, then this seems to imply that if you sin you cannot be born of God. At that time I for one certainly could not understand how this could be the case. Luckily for me I found a way out of this predicament through biblical translation. One of the things that was popular when I was studying Greek was to try to bring out the nuances of the text through the intricacies of Greek verbs. Because the verbs were in the perfective state, I found a way to make the text more palatable to my experience and actually came up with pretty much the same translation as the NIV. Through the use of translation and interpretation I was able to make the passage say that those who are born of God will not *continue* to sin. Armed with such a translation, I would be able to explain that people might continue to sin until the day they die and go to heaven. This translation certainly fit my experience but it also darkened the glorious truth of God's word. Now that I see things in a new light, I could translate the scripture in another way that would bring out the nuance of the Greek and be very encouraged by its brutality as well. The passage could just as easily be translated:

> "Whoever has been born of God does not ever sin, for his seed remains in him, and he can never sin, because he has been born of God!"

This translation absolutely excites me now. It is an incredible testimony of what Christ has worked in us through His death and resurrection. There is actually a part in us now that actually cannot sin. It is the life of Christ in us. We received it when we were born again. We became children of God; we received spiritual DNA. We may live our whole life and never see it come to maturity, but that seed has in it the potential to completely reproduce the life of Christ. That is the truth of God's Word. Let us go on a little journey and examine some scriptures that testify of this life.

> "But as many as received Him, to them He gave the right to become children of God, to those who believe in His name: who were born, not of blood, nor of the will of the flesh, nor of the will of man, but of God." (Jn 1:12-13 NKJV)

> "...having been born again, not of corruptible seed but incorruptible, through the word of God which lives and abides forever," (1 Pe 1:23 NKJV)

> "Therefore, if anyone is in Christ, he is a new creation; old things have passed away; behold, all things have become new." (2 Co 5:17 NKJV)

In these passages we see that there is a real spiritual birth that takes place when we come to Christ. We literally become a new creation from an incorruptible seed. Before we come to Christ we are only sons of Adam. When we are born again we become something completely new; we become sons of God. This is the glory of the new covenant! This is why those who are least in the kingdom of heaven are greater than John the Baptist. This is the restoration of what was lost in the fall: we lost our spiritual life in the fall of man and were left with only carnal life. During the old covenant people were only forgiven on the grounds of the promise, now we can be born again! The old covenant only had forgiveness of sin; the new covenant includes deliverance from sin. In the old covenant, people were only able to minister in the outer and inner courts. The holy of holies was not yet made open to man. There was incredible glory revealed in people who had access to the outer and inner courts, yet, compared to the new covenant, it was only a shadow. In the old covenant we have the servants of God; in the new covenant we have the sons. It was an incredible affront to the devil to have the Jewish Nation on the earth, who were servants in the house of God rather than slaves in the house of sin under his power. The fulfillment of God's plan, however, was to bring forth from the Jews the one who would populate the earth with sons of God.

"And so it is written, "The first man Adam became a living being." The last Adam became a life-giving spirit." (1 Co 15:45 NKJV)

Adam was originally created a son of God and he was given dominion over the earth. Everything was different in the days before the fall of man. Even creation itself was different. The moment Adam ate of the tree of the knowledge of Good and evil, he died. Spiritually he died and later he physically died as a result of being spiritually dead. He became the father of the race of men, born spiritually dead. Every tree gives birth after its own kind. Frogs give birth to frogs, eagles give birth to eagles and spiritually dead Adam gave birth to spiritually dead people. Yet God gave Adam a promise in Gen 3:15 that there would come a seed who would crush the serpents head and restore men to paradise. Everything in history until the cross, God intentionally governed in order to fulfill this covenantal promise. God worked through Israel as a covenantal people whom God used to bring this promise to pass. Sure, people of all times could write their history books, but God had His eye on this one thing alone: to fulfill His promise to Adam to restore what was lost in the fall.

"Therefore, just as through one man sin entered the world, and death through sin, and thus death spread to all men, because all sinned— (For until the law sin was in the world, but sin is not imputed when there is no law. Nevertheless death reigned from Adam to Moses, even over those who had not sinned according to the likeness of the transgression of Adam, who is a type of Him who was to come." (Ro 5:12-14 NKJV)

You will notice that scripture declares that all sinned through Adam. Also notice that even before the law, which refers to the law given by Moses to Israel, death reigned. The kingdom where death reigns is the kingdom of darkness. People are born into this kingdom because they are descendants of Adam. Biblically it is clear that sin is passed through the father to the children and not through the mother. This is how Jesus was able to be a sinless man. He had a sinful human mother, but because He had no human father, He was able to be born without sin! He truly is the sinless son of God and the son of man! Jesus, who was without sin died on the cross for our sins. He made complete atonement for sin! He truly took away the sin of the world! Through His death He brought an end to the reign of sin and death. He took away all grounds of the curse. He took back all the dominion that had been given through Adam to the devil. Through His death He became a life giving spirit! Through faith in Him we literally are born again sons of God! Just like Jesus came into a sinful human being through Mary, so also when we are born again His life comes into us. Just like Jesus, that spiritual man needs to grow until it comes to maturity and then the kingdom of God will be manifested.

> "For though you might have ten thousand instructors in Christ, yet you do not have many fathers; for in Christ Jesus I have begotten you through the gospel." (1 Co 4:15 NKJV)

Through faith in the gospel of Jesus Christ people are born again.

> "...that if you confess with your mouth the Lord Jesus and believe in your heart that God

has raised Him from the dead, you will be saved. For with the heart one believes unto righteousness, and with the mouth confession is made unto salvation." (Ro 10:9-10 NKJV)

There are many churches that this is as far as their experience goes. It is all about getting people born again. The glorious truth is that being born again is just the beginning. When we are born again we are a newborn babe in Christ. We have the potential to grow up to be like Jesus, but we need the right context in which to grow. If a couple has a baby and leaves it out in the woods, that baby is going to die. I remember having dreams where I was pressing through a room full of babies that were on life support, and I was striving to break out the other side. I feel this is a great description of much of the church. We can be born again for 80 years, living as a Christian, and still die a babe in Christ! We also have potential to come to maturity in Christ.

"Now I say that the heir, as long as he is a child, does not differ at all from a slave, though he is master of all, but is under guardians and stewards until the time appointed by the father. Even so we, when we were children, were in bondage under the elements of the world. But when the fullness of the time had come, God sent forth His Son, born of a woman, born under the law, to redeem those who were under the law, that we might receive the adoption as sons. And because you are sons, God has sent forth the Spirit of His Son into your hearts, crying out, "Abba, Father!" Therefore you are no longer a slave but a son, and if a son, then an heir of God through Christ." (Ga 4:1-7 NKJV)

This scripture is true at many levels. One level is the simple principle that as long as an heir is a child, he does not differ at all from a slave. We may be heirs of God through Christ, but as long as we are in immaturity we appear as slaves rather than as heirs. This has been the experience around which many Christians have built their theology. We need to build our theology around the Word and let our experience come into obedience. Many Christians have experienced life in immaturity and expected that was all there is to the faith. Their experience is that they are in bondage to sin but it is okay because they are forgiven and will go to heaven. It is true that a baby Christian will have a lot of carnality and that is okay when we are a spiritual baby, but the good news is God wants us to grow up. We need to see the heirs of God come to maturity.

"And He Himself gave some to be apostles, some prophets, some evangelists, and some pastors and teachers, for the equipping of the saints for the work of ministry, for the edifying of the body of Christ, till we all come to the unity of the faith and of the knowledge of the Son of God, to a perfect man, to the measure

39

of the stature of the fullness of Christ;" (Eph 4:11-13 NKJV)

"...the mystery which has been hidden from ages and from generations, but now has been revealed to His saints. To them God willed to make known what are the riches of the glory of this mystery among the Gentiles: which is Christ in you, the hope of glory. Him we preach, warning every man and teaching every man in all wisdom, that we may present every man perfect in Christ Jesus. To this end I also labor, striving according to His working which works in me mightily." (Col 1:26-29 NKJV)

Observe what the focus of Paul's ministry and the focus of God's ministry through apostles, prophets, evangelists, pastors and teachers is: it is to bring the people of God to maturity. Being a father and mother is much more than being able to create a child; it is lifelong role. This is God's primary agenda. I wonder what things would be like if the church invested as much time, money, and energy to mature Christians as it does to create them. One of the saddest realities in the church is that after many make a commitment to Christ in a crusade, there are often few abiding in Christ of the vast numbers reported a year later. We need to see many people come to Christ, but if we do not invest in the structure of church, there will be nowhere to nurture people to maturity. As the church begins to invest in fullness of biblical discipleship, there will be many more people coming to Christ, and there will be more who continually abide in Christ. There will also be incredible manifestations of the kingdom of God. All of this will certainly take place in the church as we structure according to God's priorities. More importantly, God will see to it that the church fulfills the mission Jesus gave it. The children of God will come to maturity on the earth; God will complete the work He began when we instituted the church.

I remember well a season in my life that began when I was reading through scripture and realized that I went quickly over scriptures that I didn't understand. I was reading through the first chapter of Ephesians and I realized I didn't understand what was meant by "God has blessed us with every spiritual blessing in heavenly places in Christ." It was that simple past tense that bugged me. Here it says that He has already blessed us with every blessing. Sure, I had experienced many wonderful blessings but certainly not every blessing. What made it worse was how excited Paul seemed about it all. It was clear that God had already done it, and therefore I wanted to enjoy it, but it was little more than a head buzz to me. As I sat pondering this passage, I decided I could not figure it out on my own, so I did something that opened up a whole new life in Christ to me. I asked God to show me what it meant. Now it didn't happen immediately, not even that day, but a few days later as I was going about my normal life it was like a flash of lightning struck my mind. I suddenly could see it and came to understand that scripture in a much deeper way. What got me more excited was the simple realization that if I needed understanding all I had to do was ask. I was so excited that I started reading through the scripture and every part I didn't understand I asked God to give me understanding. It was an exciting time in my life! God honors childlike faith. It actually became almost comical. I remember reading:

> "For there are three that bear witness in heaven: the Father, the Word, and the Holy Spirit; and these three are one. And there are three that bear witness on earth: the Spirit, the water, and the blood; and these three agree as one." (1 Jn 5:7-8 NKJV)

I prayed God would reveal this one to me, and I thought, "aha, here is a toughy." A couple of days after I prayed to understand this scripture, a Christian brother wrote me from another country and actually asked me to explain to him what this scripture meant. I thought "this is ridiculous, not coincidence." I didn't write him back for about a month, and he probably thought I was being rude. The simple truth was I had no idea what it meant. Then one day while I was preaching, I could suddenly see what this scripture meant, and boy I got excited. There was one scripture during this time that transformed my life forever.

> "For I consider that the sufferings of this present time are not worthy to be compared with the glory which shall be revealed in us.

For the earnest expectation of the creation
eagerly waits for the revealing of the sons
of God. For the creation was subjected to
futility, not willingly, but because of Him
who subjected it in hope; because the creation
itself also will be delivered from the bondage
of corruption into the glorious liberty of the
children of God." (Ro 8:18-21 NKJV)

All of creation is waiting eagerly for the revealing
of the Sons of God. It will be delivered from the
bondage of corruption when the sons of God are
revealed. All of creation is waiting for those who are
born again to be revealed or manifested as they actually are, the sons of God. Just like Jesus was revealed
as the son of God when He came to maturity, so will
Christians be when they come to maturity. He is truly
the first born of many sons.

You will notice that you see no difference in
the manifestation of the Kingdom of God under
the ministry of Peter, John, Paul and many others
from that of Jesus. They were reproduced as sons.
I want to make it clear that for all eternity we will
be searching the unsearchable riches of Christ. We
will always be growing. Just because a person comes
to maturity doesn't mean that they stop growing. It
simply means that they are now an adult and are able
to join in their father's business. If you study Jesus
for example, you will see that he went on from His
baptism at the Jordon River to greater works all the
way to the cross and into resurrection life. There was
quite a transformation between the time Jesus came

back from the wilderness after being baptized in the Jordon and Jesus on Easter morning. In a sense, coming to maturity is another type of beginning- rather than an end. In every way we see in Jesus the pattern of the sons of God.

I remember when I was a new Christian. I would always pray to be like Peter, John, or Paul. That was as far as I could see. I would always think that they are men and Jesus is God. Jesus was too high of a target to aim for. This kind of thinking is contrary to scripture in every way. I am not called to be conformed to the image of Peter, or John, or Paul but into the image of Christ, just as they were. We actually have the potential to be conformed into the image of Christ. It is all in the seed that we received when we were born again. It is who we actually are, but we need to grow up. We need to invest in God's agenda, restore biblical discipleship and grow into our full potential in Christ. God is at work bringing this to pass, and it will come to pass before the end. It is promised in Scripture, which cannot lie. Praise Jesus!

The Kingdom Reign

The book of Romans has been for many people the starting point for a spiritual revolution. I grew up in the Lutheran Church on stories of the great conversion of Martin Luther from reading Romans. Years later I discovered that Wesley also had his turning point through reading Romans. While the passage I shared with you previously was revolutionary to me, it was the culmination of an awakening that began in me through the book of Romans.

Again it was through wrestling with a scripture that seemed out of place.

> "I find then a law, that evil is present with me, the one who wills to do good. For I delight in the law of God according to the inward man. But I see another law in my members, warring against the law of my mind, and bringing me into captivity to the law of sin which is in my members. O wretched man that I am! Who will deliver me from this body of death? I thank God—through Jesus Christ our Lord!

So then, with the mind I myself serve the law
of God, but with the flesh the law of sin." (Ro
7:21-25 NKJV)

What in the world is the "I thank God-through
Jesus Christ our Lord!"? What is Paul giving thanks
for? Let us try to piece it together. Paul cries out "O
wretched man that I am! Who will deliver me from
this body of death?" I see the question in scripture,
but what about the answer? Don't try to tell me that
he is thanking God that he is serving the law of sin.
Ridiculous! Many try to fit this into their theology
like this: *even though we want to do good, we never
will this side of eternity. But, thank God that there is
no condemnation because we are forgiven because
of the cross.* Such an interpretation also has to be
imposed upon the text. I have no problem with that
if it lines up with the text and the rest of scripture,
but boy it feels like you are trying to cram a round
peg through a square hole. It still doesn't answer
the question of "who will deliver me from this body
of death?" It turns a climax around into a meager
fizzle.

Understanding the Greek, and that originally there
were no chapters and verses in scripture, I am going
to offer you a possible translation of this passage.
I want to make it clear that the argument that I am
about to make in no way rests on a new translation
because it will be clear from the rest of the testimony
of Romans and all of scripture. I am just offering it to
you for your edification.

Paul is going through Romans and presenting the gospel of the Kingdom of God. The great kingdom question is who is king? Whoever is king makes the law, and that law governs the way things are. Paul wonderfully describes what it is like under the law of sin and death. It is the law belonging to the kingdom of darkness that governs the old creation, and it always will. It is the law that reigns even in that shadow of the new covenant. It reigned in all who were under the grace of the old covenant. It is the law where the good we want to do we are unable to do because of sin living in us. The old covenant was all about being forgiven of sins. In the new covenant we are saved from our sins. We are saved from the law of sin and death. We are delivered from bondage into the spiritual freedom of the sons of God. The gospel of the kingdom is good news indeed!

The translation that I propose is this:

"O wretched man that I am, who will deliver me from this body of death which with the mind serves the law of God but with the flesh serves the law of sin? Thanks be to God that through Jesus Christ our Lord He has done this very thing!"

I challenge you to read this translation and go straight into Romans 8 to see if you don't join with Paul and shout "hallelujah!"

"There is therefore now no condemnation to those who are in Christ Jesus, who do not walk according to the flesh, but according to the Spirit. For the law of the Spirit of life in Christ Jesus has made me free from the law of sin and death. For what the law could not do in that it was weak through the flesh, God did by sending His own Son in the likeness of sinful flesh, on account of sin: He condemned sin in the flesh, that the righteous requirement of the law might be fulfilled in us who do not walk according to the flesh but according to the Spirit." (Ro 8:1-4 NKJV)

I like the textus receptus inclusion of the clause "who do not walk according to the flesh but according to the Spirit." I think it wonderfully connects with the whole of scripture, but again it is still unnecessary to prove what Paul is teaching. Practically speaking, many who are truly born again experience condemnation when they walk in the flesh and do not when they walk in the Spirit, so I find it a very helpful clause.

The glorious proclamation is: Jesus Christ is Lord! There is a new king with a new law. It is the law of the spirit of life in Christ Jesus. What the law couldn't do because of the weakness of the flesh God has done for us by sending Jesus. The law told us that we should walk in love towards God and one another, but all it proved is that we are incapable to do so. Praise God that from the very beginning with Adam He has been covering our transgression with the shedding of blood. He was looking to the day when Jesus died on the cross. The glory of the covenant with Israel was the forgiveness of sins. The glory of the new covenant is deliverance from sin. The law told us to walk in love and provided forgiveness because we couldn't. The gospel empowers us to walk in love and provides covering as we are growing up. The righteous requirement of the law is fulfilled in us who walk according to the Spirit.

> "I say then: Walk in the Spirit, and you shall not fulfill the lust of the flesh." (Ga 5:16 NKJV)

It is that simple; if you walk in the Spirit you will not fulfill the desires of the flesh.

The foundations of this glorious kingdom gospel were laid earlier in Romans and they always go back to the cross.

> "Knowing this, that our old man was crucified with Him, that the body of sin might be done away with, that we should no longer be slaves of sin. For he who has died has been freed from sin. Now if we died with Christ, we believe that we shall also live with Him," (Ro 6:6-8 NKJV)

Listen to the proclamations:

1. Our old man was crucified.
2. The body of sin is done away with.
3. We are no longer slaves: we have been freed from sin.

These are bold proclamations of victory through Jesus. The body of sin, that part of us which was a slave to sin has actually died. We are a new creation. The old man has passed away. It all happened at the cross.

"Therefore, my brethren, you also have become dead to the law through the body of Christ, that you may be married to another— to Him who was raised from the dead, that we should bear fruit to God. For when we were in the flesh, the sinful passions which were aroused by the law were at work in our members to bear fruit to death. But now we have been delivered from the law, having died to what we were held by, so that we should serve in the newness of the Spirit and not in the oldness of the letter." (Ro 7:4-6 NKJV)

Through our union with the body of Christ when we were born again, we died to the law that was against us. We became divorced from the kingdom of darkness and are now married to another. We are now united with Christ. Every tree bears fruit according to its kind. This is why the glory of the old covenant always had to fade. It was impossible to bear the fruit of the Spirit until we are born again and walk in the Spirit. Spiritual fruit is simply a manifestation of our spiritual DNA. We bear fruit according to what we are in Christ; sons of God.

Romans 8 contains teaching on how to walk in the Spirit and then continues with this:

"But you are not in the flesh but in the Spirit, if indeed the Spirit of God dwells in you. Now if anyone does not have the Spirit of Christ, he is not His. And if Christ is in you, the body is dead because of sin, but the Spirit is life because of righteousness. But if the Spirit of Him who raised Jesus from the dead dwells in you, He who raised Christ from the dead will also give life to your mortal bodies through His Spirit who dwells in you." (Ro 8:9-11 NKJV)

Here we see that we are not in the flesh but in the Spirit if the Spirit of God dwells in us. Paul is not referring to being born again. He tells us that if Christ is in us (which is being born again) then the body is dead because of sin but the spirit is alive because of Righteousness. Therefore we see that a person can be born again and actually still be carnal and full of sin. Then it goes on to say that if the Spirit of Him who raised Jesus from the dead dwells in you, He who raised Christ from the dead will also give life to your mortal bodies through His Spirit who dwells in you. This is a glorious truth: we can actually have the Spirit that raised Jesus from the dead in us and giving life to our death-doomed mortal bodies! It is absolutely impossible that the Spirit of the resurrection should dwell in us and we would not know it, or that it wouldn't revolutionize everything. That is what it does. It revolutionizes everything. We no longer find ourselves trapped doing the very sinful things that we hate, but we actually find ourselves empowered to walk in love and free from the power of sin and death.

The reason I went through these scriptures is because all of this teaching has had a very practical impact in my life and many others that I have known. Simply put, I am able to proclaim with boldness that Jesus will set you free from the entire curse of sin and death. Such a message does not heap condemnation on those who find themselves trapped and in bondage by things that they hate but rather gives them hope for liberty. It is wonderful when people hear the gospel of the kingdom and believe it and become free! It is a message of full salvation in Jesus Christ. Such faith results in a manifestation of the victory of Jesus upon the cross. This is preaching Christ crucified. Such a gospel has set a person free from addictions to pornography, drugs, depression, anger, bitterness, and anything else that is part of the government of sin and death. Every day I witness the revolutionary impact of the gospel of the kingdom of God in people's lives.

Such a gospel takes evangelism to a whole new level. I actually believe that Jesus will set people free from whatever is holding them in bondage. I do not believe it happens as people do what they are told they should and should not do, but as people enter into the presence of God because of the blood of Jesus. As we fix our eyes on Jesus and come to actually know Him (and not just about Him) such relational knowledge of God will actually transform our lives and set us free from everything of the kingdom of sin and death.

I know by experience that sometimes when people hear these truths they have an immediate spiritual revolution, but most begin with a hope that their situation will change and eventually grow into it. It is a message of hope and freedom, and it literally brings forth a people who overflow with spiritual life. Sure, we often find that we can experience spiritual freedom in some areas while we have other areas of our life that are not yet submitted to Jesus. The good news is that Jesus has already delivered us through the cross from all bondage to sin and death. As we walk with Him, He will extend His reign over every area of our lives. Even the hope of freedom is much more beautiful than being trapped in hopelessness.

Everything that Jesus gave us through His death and resurrection becomes real through faith. Forgiveness of sin, fellowship with the Spirit, power not to sin, healing, deliverance, and all of the life of Christ is available, but it only becomes experiential through faith. Many times my faith is not yet mature enough to actually posses what I know to be true in scripture. I had a dream where I was in a room with a man talking about the kingdom, and he said to me that I needed to get truth from my head into my heart. At first I was offended, but then I realized it was just an invitation to life. There is far more to experience than I have already experienced. I have experienced some wonderful things in Jesus Christ, but there are so many more things to experience! The Holy Spirit takes all that belongs to Jesus and declares it to us. The more Jesus is revealed to us, the more we will become like Him. Instead of feeling condemned, discouraged, or as a failure because of what I lack, I am excited and expectant for the life of Christ to be revealed in me. When I see areas that fall short of the glory of God I do not doubt how much God loves me, nor do I magnify my faults and failures. I just eagerly look to Jesus and rejoice that my destiny is to be conformed into His image.

> "For *"whoever calls* on the name of the Lord shall be saved." How then shall they call on Him in whom they have not believed? And how shall they believe in Him of whom they have not heard? And how shall they hear without a preacher? And how shall they preach unless they are sent? As it is written: *"How beautiful are the feet of those who preach the gospel of peace, Who bring glad tidings of good things!"* But they have not all obeyed the gospel. For Isaiah says, *"Lord, who has believed our report?"* So then faith *comes* by hearing, and hearing by the word of God." (Ro 10:13-17 NKJV)

The pattern is simple: First we hear, then we believe, and then we are saved. We have to hear the word of God in order to believe in it. In believing, we will have what is promised. This is why I get excited when I hear or see something I never saw before about Jesus when it is in agreement with scriptures. I know that in the right context, the truth will grow in me until it has given birth. I hear the word of God, I hope in the word of God, and when I come to the place of faith, I experience what the word has promised. This is the pattern of faith that scripture testifies to. Look at Abraham, God gave him a promise that he would be the father of many nations when he and his wife were too old for this to physically happen.

> "...who, contrary to hope, in hope believed, so that he became the father of many nations, according to what was spoken, *"So shall your descendants be."* And not being weak in faith, he did not consider his own body, already dead (since he was about a hundred years old), and the deadness of Sarah's womb. He did not waver at the promise of God through unbelief, but was strengthened in faith, giving glory to God, and being fully convinced that what He had promised He was also able to perform." (Ro 4:18-21 NKJV)

We see that Abraham heard the promise of God and hoped in it despite all of the circumstances that seemed contrary to the truth of God's word. Yet, until his faith became mature, his son remained in the womb of hope. Notice it says that Abraham "contrary to hope, in hope believed." He wrestled with his hope until his faith became mature. Then Sarah conceived and gave birth to Isaac, the son God promised. If Abraham would have wavered at the promise of God through unbelief, then the promise that he was pregnant with would have been aborted.

Here is the pattern again. First we need to hear the Word of God. That sounds obvious, but all too often we reject to Word of God that would impregnate us with life because it doesn't fit with what we currently believe. God wants us to grow, but it requires more revelation of Jesus. He wants to grow the garden of God so that it yields many fruits. Each fruit has its own seed. It is all completely contained in the one seed which is Christ, but there are many aspects of the Word of God that, when we believe, will bring forth more of the life of Christ in us. When people reject such words from God it becomes like the seed that falls on the path, which the birds of the air eat up.

Once we accept the seed of the Word of God we need to carry that seed in hope as our faith matures. At this point we have to contend with everything all around us that seems to contradict what the Word says. The seed is fighting to get its roots into us so that the trials and tribulations of this world do not kill it. All of this is still not enough, we need to give birth. We need to wrestle with hope until we give birth by faith. At this point the battle is to care enough. So many times we are content with the promise instead of the actual substance of what we are hoping for. Until faith comes to maturity, all we have is talk. The Kingdom of God is not in talk but in power.

God wants to develop churches that are contexts for his seed to come to maturity. Some of the things that it will require are expectancy and faith. People need a longing and a hope for more revelation of Jesus that reproduces itself in God's people. We need to make a conscious effort to receive every word God speaks. When we hear something, we need to be like the Bereans, who upon hearing the gospel first preached to them by Paul, searched the scriptures to see if it lined up with God's Word. God wants churches to be places where His seed can be manifested in the flesh, our flesh. God wants to take all of the restrictions off of the body of Christ so that we will grow up into who we already are in Christ.

Holiness Preacher

—ɯ—

Iconfess it. I am a holiness preacher. But not as many expect. I preach holiness not through works of the law but through faith in the gospel. I preach it not through human discipline but through the power of the Holy Spirit. I preach it not through old covenant works but through new covenant faith in Jesus. I preach it through the revelation of Jesus Christ.

Shortly after I moved to Northern Ireland I had a series of three dreams that were very interesting to me. Two times I found myself outside of a house wrestling with a spirit of witchcraft. In the third dream I was outside the same house and this time the presence of God was absolutely overwhelming. I was actually confused in my dream, and I asked God "did I die and go to heaven." I heard Him reply, "The church has overcome the principality and now the kingdom of heaven is revealed." Well, it was a simple series of dreams that carry a lot of scriptural truth. The church is actually fighting the unseen spiritual host of wickedness. We are called to overturn their thrones and establish the throne of King Jesus.

We have a commission to plant the government of heaven on earth, which is accomplished as people come into the obedience of Christ. I do not believe we make doctrines or teachings from dreams or visions, but they are definitely an encouragement.

I sometimes laugh when I hear of people's silly mistakes. I laugh because I often see myself when people are sharing about their situations and mistakes. I laugh because, despite our mistakes and failures, Jesus is still on the throne and He still is able to accomplish His purposes. I have been blessed because I have learned many things, almost all of them from my mistakes!

Well, it would seem obvious that if you had a series of dreams like I did that the first thing you would do would be to ask God what they mean and what should be done about them. Believe it or not it took over a year before I actually asked God about them. Oh how I wish I would ask Him about things much sooner! The problem was that in my own opinion I thought I knew all about witchcraft so I didn't feel a need to ask God. (There is a wealth of teaching going around in the body of Christ about witchcraft, and it is true and helpful. For example, in the flesh witchcraft manifests itself through intimidation, manipulation, and domination. All of these are rooted in fear and insecurity.) The problem is that when we think we know it all, we don't rely on the Lord, which is a serious waste of time if I spin it in the best possible light.

Here are some things that I learned about witchcraft. One thing that witchcraft does is it robs people of life and freedom in Christ. It leaves people going through motions of religion devoid of power, peace and joy. Where it is in operation there tends to be a lack of spiritual fellowship even if people are very involved in the church. People end up feeling disconnected from God and are dissatisfied. I remember telling a pastor once that everyone in his church was disconnected. He asked me why I would think such a thing when everyone was actively engaged in some part of the church life. I explained that just because people are active in the church doesn't mean that they are actually engaged in spiritual fellowship. There can be no spiritual fellowship while people have their eyes filled with their faults and failures rather than the truth of God's word. Such people will see others as they see themselves, and it is no wonder there would be no fellowship with God or man.

Witchcraft always degenerates into a fault-finding spirit. I remember someone telling me they had the gift of discernment and then proceeded to tell me all the faults of different people in the church. While they were probably right on many points, I asked them to tell me all the good things about the same people and they couldn't tell me one good thing. I explained that when God gives discernment it actually breaks our heart for the people. It causes us to be for them and not against them. It will always bear the fruit of love. Spiritual gifts actually empower the life of Christ in one another rather than the flesh. They reveal the character of our redeemer and savior, not the thief and robber. I do not mean that they don't sometimes appear to backfire. If God calls someone to speak a word of rebuke or correction, it often times seems to put people further into their bondage, but it is actually the opportunity for them to come to freedom. The key is that spiritual gifts will bear the fruit of love rather than pride in the people who operate in them because love is the power that empowers them. I am not saying that someone who operates in spiritual gifts cannot immediately get puffed up with pride after they operate in them, but the actual gift will not operate while in that state. God will not pour His anointing upon any flesh.

I remember one time when someone was manifesting an evil spirit. They started blaspheming and cursing God. They were crying for help, saying they couldn't stop it. I knew all of the scriptures and teachings about how to cast out evil spirits and I went for it with all my might. Nothing happened. Finally something shifted in my spirit and I looked to God. My spirit basically said "Lord, I know you love this person and I know you want to deliver them from this, but I can't do it." Immediately I experienced the power of God rise up in me, my voice changed in a way where the power of God was in it, and that spirit was cast out. It was incredible. I absolutely loved it. I was a young believer and maybe sometimes when I shared that story I thought I was a very great Christian, maybe I sometimes got puffed up with pride, but the honest truth, it operated in the moment of my weakness not my pride.

When spiritual fellowship is broken in a community, people look towards all kinds of things to fill the void. It takes all kinds of forms from bitterness, busyness, complaining, gossiping, self-righteous-ness, self medicating with the things of this world or many other things that have no life in them. When communities are breaking down, whether it is in the home, the church or in society, it is because people are losing the life-giving connection with the Spirit of God and thus with one another. The foundation of true healthy fellowship among men is healthy fellow-ship with God because of the blood of Jesus. Without this relationship in place everything else falls apart.

When we are truly walking in the spirit we find that we have beautiful fellowship with those who are also walking in the spirit, but we will also often have severe conflict with those who are in the flesh. When we are in the flesh we can often find unity and fellowship around something other than the presence of God but find ourselves in conflict with anything that would expose this.

One of the primary ways that people are robbed of this vital fellowship with God that results in life-giving fellowship with man is through witchcraft. Let us look at some scriptures that deal with this.

"O foolish Galatians! Who has bewitched you that you should not obey the truth, before whose eyes Jesus Christ was clearly portrayed among you as crucified? This only I want to learn from you: Did you receive the Spirit by the works of the law, or by the hearing of faith?— Are you so foolish? Having begun in the Spirit, are you now being made perfect by the flesh? Have you suffered so many things

in vain—if indeed it was in vain? Therefore
He who supplies the Spirit to you and works
miracles among you, does He do it by the
works of the law, or by the hearing of faith?
just as Abraham "believed God, and it was
accounted to him for righteousness.'" (Ga
3:1-6 NKJV)

Notice that the Galatians were fighting with witchcraft. The primary manifestation was that they were
trying to complete in the flesh through the works of
the law what was begun in the Spirit by the hearing of
faith. Paul is passionate for these people that the life
of Christ would be unhindered in their midst. They
had begun well, but they were being tricked. They
begun with the supply of the Spirit and miracles and
now that was being restricted. Why? Because the
Spirit and the ministry of miracles operate by the
hearing of faith and not by the works of the law.

The shame of being identified with Christ is so
glorious! It is such a stumbling block that people
can barely stand the simplicity and beauty of it. We
are saved by grace through faith, not of works lest
any man should boast. It is faith that accesses the
grace that came through the death and resurrection
of Jesus.

You will often find that, humanly speaking there
is a huge cost to be identified with a true work of the
Spirit because it is absolutely humbling to our flesh.
It is a reproach to our human wisdom, power, and
ability. Yet it is the wisdom and power of God in the
midst of men. Just look at all the ways the people

of God were treated throughout the ages that paid the cost to be identified with the kingdom of God among men. Luther was brought before the most powerful men in the world and was threatened with death if he refused to compromise the gospel. Wesley was put out by the institutional church. Whitefield (a leader of the first great awakening) was mocked on the stage. The early Pentecostals were called holy rollers. All of these people paid a great price to be identified with the kingdom of God. Such identification with Jesus is true wisdom. Wisdom will be justified by her children. Such people are often rejected in life and honored in death. Their stories are endless, but the people who have paid the cost to be identified with the move of the Holy Spirit will by no means be ashamed in Eternity.

The spirit of witchcraft seeks to intimidate, manipulate, and dominate the move of the Spirit of God. It tries to make it palatable to the flesh and men, but in the end it restricts the life of Christ in us.

> "Beware lest anyone cheat you through philosophy and empty deceit, according to the tradition of men, according to the basic principles of the world, and not according to Christ. For in Him dwells all the fullness of the Godhead bodily; and you are complete in Him, who is the head of all principality and power." (Col 2:8-10 NKJV)

It wasn't just the Galatians who had to contend with witchcraft. There were people who were trying to bring the Colossians into bondage so that they could make religion more palatable to the flesh. Paul makes a bold proclamation; we are complete in Christ. Let nothing be added by men to all that God has done for us in Jesus! If you want to compete, for example, with Hindu holy men who supposedly burn at a sinner's touch, or Buddhists who sweep the ground before they walk on it lest they should kill an insect, go for it. See if by works of the flesh you are able to reproduce the miracles and power of the gospel of grace. You will never do it. Go ahead and see if sorcerers and magicians can contend with Moses or Elijah. In the presence of the kingdom of God they will cry out, "This is nothing other than the hand of God!"

"In Him you were also circumcised with the circumcision made without hands, by putting off the body of the sins of the flesh, by the circumcision of Christ, buried with Him in baptism, in which you also were raised with Him through faith in the working of God, who raised Him from the dead. And you, being dead in your trespasses and the uncir-cumcision of your flesh, He has made alive together with Him, having forgiven you all trespasses, having wiped out the handwriting of requirements that was against us, which was contrary to us. And He has taken it out of the way, having nailed it to the cross. Having disarmed principalities and powers, He made a public spectacle of them, triumphing over them in it." (Col 2:11-15 NKJV)

Again, it is all accomplished in preaching Christ crucified. You cannot separate that Christ was crucified from the resurrection and ascension. When we were united with Christ we were united to it all. We have become partakers of that life when we were baptized into Christ. We actually have His life available to be manifested in us today through the hearing of faith.

> "Therefore, if you died with Christ from the basic principles of the world, why, as though living in the world, do you subject yourselves to regulations— "Do not touch, do not taste, do not handle," which all concern things which perish with the using— according to the commandments and doctrines of men? These things indeed have an appearance of wisdom in self-imposed religion, false humility, and neglect of the body, but are of no value against the indulgence of the flesh." (Col 2:20-23 NKJV)

The Colossians are being tricked to try to complete in the flesh what was begun in the Spirit. Yet this is what churches are doing today. It appears to be so holy. It certainly is sincere and intended to help God. Yet it is all out of bounds in the church and it restricts the life of Christ in the people. It leaves people in bondage to their flesh.

"Beware of dogs, beware of evil workers, beware of the mutilation! For we are the circumcision, who worship God in the Spirit, rejoice in Christ Jesus, and have no confidence in the flesh," (Php 3:2-3 NKJV)

During the time that I was seeking God to teach me about witchcraft and how to overcome it, I kept having visions of dogs. I couldn't figure it out. Then one day it dawned on me; a dog is simply a sign of the flesh. They have no spiritual life, only carnal life. There are nice happy dogs, astute hunting dogs, energetic dogs, vicious dogs and many other kinds of dogs. There is something lovable about them all, yet at the end of the day they are simply dogs that only carnal life. This is what witchcraft does; it keeps us bound to our carnal nature instead of releasing us into our spiritual inheritance as sons of God!

So what is the solution? How do we see people grow into the image of Christ? How do we overcome witchcraft that leaves people bound to their carnal nature? As always, to the Word!

"But if the ministry of death, written and engraved on stones, was glorious, so that the children of Israel could not look steadily at the face of Moses because of the glory of his countenance, which glory was passing away, how will the ministry of the Spirit not be more glorious? For if the ministry of condemnation had glory, the ministry of righteousness exceeds much more in glory. For even what was made glorious had no glory in this respect, because of the glory that excels. For if what is passing away was glorious, what remains is much more glorious." (2 Co 3:7-11 NKJV)

In this passage I see two different types of religion that I call old covenant and new covenant religion. I am referring to what I see is the essence of the covenants. Summed up, the old covenant gave us a law filled with should and should nots that we are unable to keep and provided us forgiveness because we couldn't keep the law. The new covenant gives us the power to walk in love. I contend that much of Christianity today operates in an old covenant fashion rather than a new covenant fashion. We saw how old covenant religion was infiltrating the church during Paul's day, and it is still infiltrating churches today. It restricts the life of Christ in our midst.

First, old covenant religion here is referred to as the ministry of death engraved on stones. It is an external law of commandments that people work hard to try to keep. It tells people what they should and should not do. Every covenant has its own law and its own set of blessings and curses attached to whether or not people keep the law. The goal is to get people enjoying the blessings of the covenant. When people fail to experience all of the blessings associated with keeping the law, or if they experience the curses associated with breaking the law, they need to go back to the law and repent of anything that they are doing that breaks the law. The problem with the old covenant is that no matter how hard people try to keep the law, they always fail. Instead of being able to be justified by the law, they are condemned by it. This is why God wrote right into the old covenant provisions to make atonement for sin. They could have their sins forgiven so that God could dwell in their midst and bless them.

The problem that happens with Christians is that they are still trying to live by the old covenant law. Many Christians try to keep the law externally as their grounds of blessing, and if they find condemnation they go to the old covenant law to try to pin down the cause and repent according to that law. Other Christians get fed up with the self-righteousness such religion creates, or the constant frustration of failure and end up finding the heart of old covenant religion, which is the forgiveness of sins. This becomes their great bastion of orthodoxy: that we are simply sinners who are forgiven because of what Jesus has done. Yet this bastion of theology is filled with people who have no power to do what is right. There certainly is some glory in such religion, but it is only a shadow of what is actually available. When churches minister under old covenant forms it carries an old covenant glory. The problem is that old covenant glory always fades; it cannot be maintained. The good news is that Christianity is a religion that is based on a new covenant. It has a new law and a new priesthood. It has a glory that never fades but always gets brighter.

Look at the children of old covenant religion. It gave birth to Sadducees, Pharisees, and backsliders!

The Sadducees say there is no resurrection / able to the people of God. They believe tha. ... simply sinners saved by grace and though we fall we are forgiven by His grace. There is actually a level of life and glory in this. The Pharisees believe in resurrection life. They believe there has to be more than the watered down religion of the Sadducees' but they believe adherence to the old covenant law is the means to make it happen. They end up creating a religious system where if people adhere to it they feel halfway decent, but it stinks of self-righteousness and pride. Again, there is a level of life and glory in this as well. Backsliders, on the other hand, are frustrated and feel like they have been sold a false bill of goods. Many of them are fed up with powerlessness and sickened by self-righteousness. They are often tender-hearted and have given up on religion as they have experienced it. Often these people are the closest to the kingdom and come wonderfully alive when brought into a new covenant expression of Christianity.

The word testifies that the new covenant has a glory that never fades. We do not need to come to life for a season and then actually decline. That is abnormal Christianity. God has a much better purpose and plan for His sons and daughters, and the secret is revealed here:

> "Now the Lord is the Spirit; and where the Spirit of the Lord is, there is liberty. But we all, with unveiled face, beholding as in a mirror the glory of the Lord, are being transformed into the same image from glory to

glory, just as by the Spirit of the Lord." (2 Co
3:17-18 NKJV)

This is the secret to holiness. This is the secret
to freedom from the flesh. This is the secret of new
covenant power. This is the secret of resurrection
life. The ridiculous thing is that it is no secret at all.
It is clearly revealed in his Word. It was never meant
to be a secret; it is just hidden by a veil that is lifted
in Christ. This is Christian liberty. It is so simple and
beautiful. As we see Him we become like Him. We
will go from glory to glory as we continue to receive
more and more revelation of Him. We are always
growing but only to the extent that we are seeing
Him. We need to get into his presence in order to see
Him. Therefore, forgiveness of sins is foundational
to the new covenant as well as the old covenant. We
have access into the presence of God on the grounds
of the shed blood of Jesus, but now we have access
all the way into the holy of holies. We have access
into that which was impossible in the old covenant.
We enter into the holy of holies by the blood of Jesus,
and as we have fellowship with God as our Father,
the life of Christ that is in our new DNA is able to
grow up until we actually become conformed into
His image. To restrict this possibility in any way is to
be robbed of life.

Life in the Spirit

—⁓—

For many years I have prayed with people in corporate prayer meetings and it is absolute drudgery if the presence of the Lord is not encountered. So much of Christianity is about getting the spirit right so that the presence of God is actually encountered. I know of people who spend much time in prayer, but I wonder if they ever get into the presence of God. Their countenance is sour and there is no light in their eyes. When someone gets into the presence of God there is an incredible life-giving transfer that takes place.

I remember one person in particular who told me that she prays for hours every day. I didn't see the fruit of prayer in her life, so I told her "I bet you pray every day laying face down on your bed."

"Yeah, how did you know?"

"Just a lucky guess. I bet you spend hours begging God to forgive your sins."

"Yeah, how did you know?"

"Just a lucky guess. Next time you go to pray just try this; stand up, lift your hands toward heaven and begin praying along these lines: I thank you God because Jesus died on the cross for my sins, and because of what He has done I am forgiven."

The next time I saw her she told me "Bill, what happened? I did what you said and something wonderful started bubbling in my stomach and I started speaking in this strange language! I feel so wonderful. The presence of God is so wonderful!" I never had told her about praying in tongues, she just stumbled upon it herself. She didn't read a book about it; she was taught by the Spirit who, when there are no restrictions, will actually lead us into all truth.

I met over coffee one time with a friend who was spending incredible amounts of time in prayer. I asked to meet with him because I noticed that his countenance was heavy. I knew that the problem had to do with carnal prayer, but I wasn't sure how to bring correction. While we were talking I asked, "do you give thanks in prayer?"

"All the time," he replied. (I figured that would be his answer)

"Have you ever experienced something that really touched you and caused you to spontaneously give thanks to God?"

He thought about the question for a while and answered, "yes."

"It didn't happen in your prayer room either, did it?"

"No."

"Where did it happen?" I asked.

"When I was playing golf and hit a really good shot. I was so pleased I gave thanks to God."

"Don't you realize that was better prayer than all of the praying you have been doing over these last days? It bears the fruit of fellowship with Jesus."

I am not against regular times of prayer, nor regular places of prayer. I have prayed daily at the same time and place for years. It is not about the context but about the substance and fruit of prayer. It has to be real.

There is one story about prayer that I have encountered numerous times over. It is so important because it is often the hindrance to great corporate manifestations of the presence of God. One day I was praying with a brother in the Lord and there was a hindrance to the presence of God. I checked myself with the Spirit, and it wasn't me, so I looked at my friend and asked, "What have you done?"

"I committed 'such and such' a sin."

"How long ago?"

"About a week."

"And you feel like you are not welcome in the presence of God because of it?"

"Yep"

"And things are only getting worse and worse, and the sin keeps increasing?"

"Yep."

"Don't you realize that the only way you are going to get free from your sin is to get into His presence on the grounds of the blood? The very thing you need is the very thing you are running from. You need to get into His presence on the grounds of the blood that was shed for you at Calvary. It is only there that you will find that the things of the flesh that were accusing you will be removed."

Then he had true kingdom repentance. He repented of trying to be justified by the law and came into the presence of God on the grounds of the blood. This is the only way to a transformed life.

Another time I was praying with this same brother and three other people. The presence of God was wonderfully present, and suddenly it disappeared. I opened up my eyes and saw that the other three were on their knees. I asked everyone one by one what they felt the spirit was saying, starting with the three on their knees. One by one the three of them testified along the lines of "the spirit of God is having me repent of my sins." Finally I asked my fourth friend what he felt the Spirit of God was saying. He testified along the lines of "I feel the Spirit is saying we are forgiven by the blood and we are welcome in His presence to worship and pray. We can call down fire from heaven." Hallelujah! The other three immediately jumped up and started praising the Lord, and we had a glorious encounter with the Spirit of God. What they actually did was a type of new covenant repentance. They were transgressing the law that we are welcome in the presence of God on the grounds of the blood. When they repented of this transgression we had a glorious prayer meeting!

There are many different things I have experienced that cause the presence of the Lord to be quenched, so I am not going to limit it to condemnation. I have seen the presence of the Lord personally lift from me many times for many reasons. One time I was engulfed in the presence of God and then for one split second I became concerned what people would think and it was gone. The moment I stepped outside of the new covenant law the connection with His power was broken and I needed new covenant repentance for loving my soul life more than His life to find refreshing. The key is that when we become disconnected from His presence and power we need to repent, but we need to go to the new covenant law rather than the old covenant law so that we can be restored to the new covenant blessing. Every covenant has its own law which contains blessings and curses. If we break the law of one covenant we will not get very far if we repent according to another. Every area that we can train ourselves to stand in new covenant obedience will cause the Kingdom of God to be manifested in power. This area of condemnation, I believe, is one of the central battles that people need to overcome once and forever.

I remember one Sunday when I was scheduled to preach at a church. A week after that service I was approached by a member of the church. They told me that, when I was ministering, the presence of God was phenomenal and people were richly blessed. The other side of that story is that on the way to preach, the enemy was throwing all my faults in my face. I normally do not advocate speaking to the devil but that morning on the way to church I couldn't help myself. I said, "devil, you are exactly right. I cannot deny anything that you are accusing me of, but devil I am completely forgiven because of the blood of Jesus. The gospel is going to be preached this morning not because I am such a great Christian but because Jesus is a great God and redeemer. He deserves to have His word proclaimed so people can experience His love and grace through faith. So you go ahead and moan all you want."

Another time, a friend of mine ministered at a church and again people testified how powerful the ministry was. Just before he went to minister he was in a big fight with his wife. When asked how he could go and minister in such a state he replied, "simply on the grounds of the blood of Jesus."

I am no advocate of sin. I hate sin, especially in my own life, but the truth is Jesus forgave all of my sins on the cross. His grace is sufficient. No one can boast about their spiritual accomplishments because they are all simply a result of the grace of God. At one time in my life the Lord made His calling in my life very clear. After a season of struggling with the flesh, I sought God intensely because I was concerned I had forfeited my calling. He reaffirmed it exactly as at first. I suddenly realized that He knew everything about me when He called me. He knew every sin and mistake I would make and yet He called me. His call carries in it the power to bring His will to pass. We serve a wonderful God who is both the author and completer of our faith.

It was during that season of wrestling with my flesh that the Lord opened up His word to me. I found incredible grace to minister on the grounds of His blood, yet I was still convinced that God had more than just forgiveness for me. I became completely fed up with trying to tell God "never again." It was only after sincerely wrestling with my failure and crying out with Paul, "O wretched man that I am is there any hope for me" that God opened up the scriptures to me. It has brought forth such fruit and blessing in my life, and in others' that I cannot even begin to share how powerful it is. If the Old covenant was glorious, how much more glorious is the new covenant! The secret of the transformation was through entering His presence on the grounds of the blood of Jesus and not trying to clean myself up through the letter of the law. Before long I discovered that I was enjoying God's presence, and the things that seemed to be so hard to overcome were no longer an issue. Praise Jesus!

Let us look at some scriptures for this:

"Now when these things had been thus prepared, the priests always went into the first part of the tabernacle, performing the services. But into the second part the high priest went alone once a year, not without blood, which he offered for himself and for the people's sins committed in ignorance; the Holy Spirit indicating this, that the way into the Holiest of All was not yet made manifest while the first tabernacle was still standing. It was symbolic for the present time in which both gifts and sacrifices are offered which cannot make him who performed the service perfect in regard to the conscience— concerned only with foods and drinks, various washings, and fleshly ordinances imposed until the time of reformation." (Heb 9:6-10 NKJV)

The present time refers to the time that the sacrifices were going on. It was a time when the sacrifices that were being offered were not able to make those who offered them perfect in regard to conscience. It was the time when the way into the holy of holies was closed off to man. Man was separated from the glory of God. It was the time of the old covenant. This passage anticipates a time when the holy of holies would be open to man, a time where people are made perfect in regard to conscience. It was looking for the time of reformation. It looks to a time where man is reformed, formed again, or in other words born again as sons of God.

"For the law, having a shadow of the good things to come, and not the very image of the things, can never with these same sacrifices, which they offer continually year by year, make those who approach perfect. For then would they not have ceased to be offered? For the worshipers, once purified, would have had no more consciousness of sins. But in those sacrifices there is a reminder of sins every year." (Heb 10:1-3 NKJV)

The shadow of the new covenant was glorious, yet it could not make men perfect. The way to the holy of holies was not yet open. The first Christians actually called themselves followers of the way. The way where? Into the holy of holies. When Jesus was crucified the veil in the temple was torn. The way into the presence of God is now open. Christianity is about people entering into the presence of God and worshipping in Spirit and truth. It is by being in His presence and seeing Him that we become like Him. So many Christians get it backwards and try so hard to make themselves holy so that they feel they can come into the presence of God. This kind of religion will always leave us as failures. New covenant religion will transform us. We enter His presence on the grounds of the blood of Jesus and are delivered from our sin as we see Him.

So much of religion today is about feeling guilty. We almost get a sort of sanctimonious buzz when we fix our eyes on all of our faults and offer daily sacrifices. Being led by the Spirit is a far better way. The blood of Jesus removes all consciousness of sin when we walk in the Spirit. We may not actually be perfect but we walk in perfect communion with the Lord and as we do we are transformed into His image. There is an incredible kingdom reality that is revealed when people walk in the Spirit.

I remember an experience that made a strong impression on me. By the grace of God we had a community of people who walked in the presence of God because of the blood of Jesus. One night we ordered pizza, and a Muslim man delivered the pizza. He came into the room where we were setting up to eat, and he started prophesying. He said, "You need to pray for me. The spirit of God is in this place. The spirit of Holiness is in this place." Hallelujah! There is a very real presence of God that is meant to be manifested with His people, and it will be when we walk in the Spirit.

Walking in the Spirit must be the goal that we have for people. It is such a powerful and successful way. I remember visiting a church one time that was preaching about all of the things we should do in order to be a husband. At the end we were given a prayer to pray every day, and it was a full page front and back. Afterwards, many people were raving about how wonderful it was. I was distressed. Someone asked me what I thought. I told them that quite honestly, I couldn't keep all that stuff in my head, and if that is what I have to do to fulfill my responsibility as a husband, I wouldn't know where to begin for every other role I play in life. That way is too hard for me and burns me out. I found a better way: always maintain fellowship with His presence. As soon as communion with His presence is broken then seek Him for the cause and repent. Do not try to live by the letter of the law. We have been delivered from principalities and powers of darkness, and we have also been delivered from principle-based religion. There always seems to be 10 principles for this and 20 principles for that and 100 other things added daily with principles to achieve a desired result. It is much easier to simply have our minds renewed by the Word illuminated by His Spirit. To be led by the Spirit!

I remember one time when I was first married and felt that my wife Stephanie was being unfair. I decided I would give her a taste of her own medicine and instead of resolving the issue I let the sun go down on my anger. I felt justified in my actions. (It was totally the wrong spirit and I was being led by the flesh.) I was troubled that whole night, and the next morning the presence of God was nowhere to be found. Therefore I sought the Lord because I wanted His fellowship. As I prayed, the Lord brought scripture to my mind and I realized that I had sinned and grieved the Holy Spirit. I didn't have the right to step out of love and still expect the Holy Spirit to abide with me. I repented and His presence was restored.

If we were much more sensitive to His presence in our life and started with the assumption that communion is the normal state of the Christian, then we would have a radically different Christianity. Such Christianity would cause a great manifestation of the kingdom of God and would liberate multitudes from spiritual bondage.

> "And every priest stands ministering daily and offering repeatedly the same sacrifices, which can never take away sins. But this Man, after He had offered one sacrifice for sins forever, sat down at the right hand of God, from that time waiting till His enemies are made His footstool. For by one offering He has perfected forever those who are being sanctified." (Heb 10:11-14 NKJV)

> "...and that He may send Jesus Christ, who was preached to you before, whom heaven must receive until the times of restoration

of all things, which God has spoken by the mouth of all His holy prophets since the world began." (Ac 3:20-21 NKJV)

Jesus offered Himself once and perfected forever all who are being sanctified. He is seated at the right hand of God until all of His enemies are made His footstool. The last enemy that will be put under His feet is death (1 Cor. 15:26). Death is the seed of sin perfected. Even death will be destroyed by the kingdom of God. Every enemy is actively being put under the feet of Jesus right now. Just as when Adam sinned it took a while before he died in the body, so the same is true with the salvation brought forth when Jesus died for our sins. The blood of Jesus actually destroyed every work of the devil. All the power of sin and death has been destroyed, the entire curse has been destroyed, and all the power of darkness is already destroyed at the cross. This victory is going to be revealed on the earth as His church comes to maturity. Jesus is seated at the right hand of God, and all of His enemies are being put under His feet. Through our union with Him in baptism we are His body, and God is actually working right now to put every enemy under the feet of the church. This will be manifested as people enter His presence on the grounds of the blood and come to know him relationally more and more.

"Therefore, brethren, having boldness to enter the Holiest by the blood of Jesus, by a new and living way which He consecrated for us, through the veil, that is, His flesh, and having a High Priest over the house of God, let us draw near with a true heart in full assurance of faith, having our hearts sprinkled from an evil conscience and our bodies washed with pure water. Let us hold fast the confession of our hope without wavering, for He who promised is faithful. And let us consider one another in order to stir up love and good works, not forsaking the assembling of ourselves together, as is the manner of some, but exhorting one another, and so much the more as you see the Day approaching." (Heb 10:19-25 NKJV)

Praise Jesus that there is a living way for us to enter the holy of holies by the blood of Jesus! We need to access this boldly by His grace and draw near in full assurance of faith. Although we all have to personally respond to Jesus and engage personally with the Holy Spirit, Christianity is a communal religion-not primarily a personal one. Every one of us is where we are because of those who have invested the kingdom life in us personally. Because of the access we have by faith into the presence of God we are called to stir one another up to love and good works, and not forsake the assembling of ourselves together. Life in the Spirit is to be lived out in community, and spiritual community invigorates our life in the Spirit. Such communion with God and one another is the primary architecture of biblical church. This is the context where the spiritual DNA we received when we were born again comes to maturity. It is only in spiritual fellowship that we become conformed into the image of Christ.

A City in the trees

—ⵑ—

Early on as a Christian I had a dream of a city built in the trees. The city was very large and it was clear that a lot of time and investment had gone into building this city. As I walked through the streets of this city suspended over the earth, I became very disturbed because the roads were extremely narrow and the guard rail barely reached to my knees. I thought to myself that this was a very stupid design because it makes it very easy for people to fall to the earth and die. As I was pondering this, I suddenly realized that the whole city was designed for children. Then I blurted out loud "this whole city is designed to keep people in immaturity!" As soon as I made this proclamation, a door opened and all of the rulers of the city came against me. They asked me if I had a problem with it. Because of how intimidating these men were, I was about to put my head down and concede that I had no problem with the way it was built. Just before I submitted to them, the sovereignty of God caused a crisis in my life, so instead of staying in the city, I proclaimed that I was getting out of there, and so I did. I wandered through the wilderness, and after a series of events, a small group of believers came together who were of one heart and mind and. Then I saw the army of God assembling in mass upon the hills.

First of all, I share this because I believe that much of the church is designed to keep people in immaturity. Secondly, because I believe that there is a move of God upon the earth right now that is working powerfully to bring the church to maturity. Just as the city I saw in my dream was designed so that people would fall to the earth, so much of the church is designed so that people fall from the spiritual into the carnal. It is set up for people to fail. It is no surprise to me when believers fall into all kinds of sins of the flesh because the church has been designed in a way where that is their inheritance. It was never intended to be this way, and it doesn't have to be this way. I believe that believers are bringing to completion the work begun in the reformation. The church is being restored to what it was at the beginning, a reproduction of the life of Christ in men.

The experience of Christianity for many believers is often very unfortunate. We have inherited forms and systems that often set people up for failure. I remember speaking with a pastor of a church where the head pastor was removed because he had an affair with a member of the congregation. They were busy putting bylaws into their constitution in order to try to keep this from happening again. I tried to explain that their bylaws wouldn't do a bit of good because there were fundamental issues that set people up for failure. For example, the pastoral theology of that particular body teaches that pastors are not to have friends among the congregation because it would appear that they were showing favorites. Therefore they will be disconnected from life. They will be expected to have it all together but they are restricted from having what they need to succeed. They have no real spiritual fellowship with other believers. They are expected to come in like a business expert and run the machine, but in the end the machine runs all over them. It is no wonder to me that so many people who start out as pastors end up leaving the ministry. The system was designed for their failure in many ways. It is not just the pastors either; many others are being set up for failure too. Many Christians with hearts to serve God find themselves falling into carnality that they hate.

The good news is that God has better things in store for His people. He is restoring his church to what it was at the beginning: a manifestation of sons of God. This is exactly what Jesus manifested in His ministry and it is what Christians manifest in maturity. It is what the church will eventually manifest corporately.

A good analogy for where we are at is a fishbowl. If I were to put a goldfish into a fishbowl, the goldfish would only grow to a size relative to that fish bowl, but if I were to put it into a pond it would grow to its full potential. I believe the Lord is working powerfully to reform the church so that people reach their full potential in Christ. I thank God that for all the legitimate children of God throughout the world and I thank God for all of the spiritual life that is already in manifestation, but I thank God even more that there are better days ahead. God is removing everything that has been set up to keep people from coming to maturity in Christ!

It is promised in the Word of God.

"Another parable He put forth to them, saying: "The kingdom of heaven is like a man who sowed good seed in his field; but while men slept, his enemy came and sowed tares among the wheat and went his way. But when the grain had sprouted and produced a crop, then the tares also appeared. So the servants of the owner came and said to him, 'Sir, did you not sow good seed in your field? How then does it have tares?' He said to them, 'An enemy has done this.' The servants said to him, 'Do you want us then to go and gather them up?' But he said, 'No, lest while you gather up the tares you also uproot the wheat with them. Let both grow together until the harvest, and at the time of harvest I will say to the reapers, "First gather together the tares and bind them in bundles to burn them, but gather the wheat into my barn."''" (Mt 13:24-30 NKJV)

Many today believe that everything on earth is going to get worse and worse until Jesus comes back. With great joy I want to proclaim that there are two seeds sown in the earth, and both will come to maturity. There is one seed growing in the earth that will get worse and worse; that is the seed of sinful man. There is another seed growing that will get better and better, and that is the seed of Christ. There were two trees in the garden, and there are two kingdoms in this world. Both are growing together until the time of harvest. As long as they are both in immaturity, you will see very little difference between them, but when they come to maturity we will see what tree they are a part of. The children of God will manifest the spiritual life that was lost in the fall of man. It is the very life that is restored in Jesus Christ.

Going all the way back to the garden, we see the first expression of the kingdom of God on earth. It was a union between heaven and earth. Everything was in harmony and it was all very good. When Adam ate the fruit of the tree of the knowledge of good and evil, that kingdom was destroyed. The reign of the kingdom of God ended and the reign of sin and death began. The kingdom of God was never again seen on earth until Jesus was baptized at the Jordan. All of the Glory of the Old Testament was only a shadow of the coming Kingdom. It was a kingdom built upon the promise of restoration and upon forgiveness through atonement. It was a covenant where God dwelt among his servants on the grounds of forgiveness, but they were still sons of men. They were not yet born from above. They only had carnal DNA not spiritual DNA.

"'"Assuredly, I say to you, among those born of women there has not risen one greater than John the Baptist; but he who is least in the kingdom of heaven is greater than he." (Mt 11:11 NKJV)

This testimony from Jesus concerning John the Baptist is absolutely incredible. Think of all the great men and women of old. Think of the roll call of faith in Hebrews 11. Think of Moses who was used by God to deliver God's people from Egypt and destroy Pharaoh and His armies in the process. Think of Elijah who, on Mount Carmel called down fire from heaven on a water soaked sacrifice and turned the hearts of the people back to the true and living God. I could go on declaring the glories of old covenant religion which was only to hold things together until the time of reformation. Among all of the old covenant heroes of faith, Jesus proclaims that none is greater than John the Baptist. Jesus goes on to proclaim that He who is least in the Kingdom of heaven is greater than John the Baptist. Why? Because John the Baptist was still a son of man; he wasn't a son of God. The kingdom that was lost in the fall of man was not restored in the old covenant; it was restored in the new covenant. Jesus was the first to proclaim that the kingdom of God is at hand. He was the first to proclaim it because he was the first spiritual man since the fall. His death has brought forth spiritual children created in His spiritual image.

The glorious gospel of the Kingdom of God is being restored in this hour. The kingdom of God is at hand, it is at hand's length, it is here now. Men are able to manifest the kingdom of God on earth. After man fell it was never seen on the earth again until

Jesus was baptized at the Jordan. Even though He was born the son of God without sin, the kingdom of God was not manifested until Jesus came to maturity. Certainly there were many marvelous things about His life before that day, but it was only after He was baptized and came back from the wilderness that the kingdom of God was manifested on earth. This manifestation of the kingdom of God threw the devil into a frenzy where he probably thought he should snuff it out at any cost. This was God's forced checkmate in two but the devil couldn't see it. Maybe the glorious manifestation of the Kingdom in the ministry of Jesus blinded him to the fact that God wanted to reproduce the very same life of Christ in many believer's lives. Maybe the only thing he could think of is "I have to put out the fire." But what the devil meant for evil the Lord had ordained for good before the foundations of the earth were laid. The decks were stacked from the beginning. The cross, who's idea was it anyway? The devil thought it was his idea, but he found out that God thought of it first. All of creation testifies that unless a grain of wheat fall into the ground and dies it abides alone, but if it dies it bears much fruit. That is what Jesus did; He died so that He might reproduce His life in us. Hallelujah! He reproduced His spiritual DNA in men. God had a plan for man when He created Him, and He is able to complete every work He begins. His plan is for us to be conformed into the image of Christ.

God promised Adam and Eve that their descendant would restore men to paradise; that he would destroy the work of the devil. In the fullness of time,

Jesus came and He made good on every promise of Scripture. He came and fulfilled all of the promises in the law and the prophets. He came and destroyed all the works of the devil. He came as man, and in Him man was restored to the dominion that was given by Adam to satan through the fall. In His death on the cross all creation was reconciled to God. The curtain that separated creation from God was rent. The way into the holy of holies was made open. The glory and communion with God that man was separated from because of sin has been fully restored through the cross of Jesus.

Jesus reconciled all of creation to God through the cross. He ascended into heaven where he remains as Lord of all until the work he completed on the cross manifests its victory over all creation. The kingdom of God will one day rule over all of the earth. Yet, after Jesus ascended into heaven, the kingdom departed again. The Kingdom of God was absent from earth- but only for ten days. On the day of Pentecost, the Kingdom of God returned to earth. That day men saw the Kingdom of God come in power.

> "And He said to them, "Assuredly, I say to you that there are some standing here who will not taste death till they see the kingdom of God present with power."" (Mk 9:1 NKJV)

Many who were in the world in Jesus' day never saw the Kingdom of God. Many who even saw Jesus in the flesh never saw the kingdom. Many around the world on the day of Pentecost never saw the kingdom. Many during the time of the first century church never saw the kingdom come in power, yet many others did. The same is true today. At Pentecost, the kingdom of God was restored upon the earth, but not everyone on earth actually sees it.

> """Most assuredly, I say to you, he who believes in Me, the works that I do he will do also; and greater works than these he will do, because I go to My Father." (Jn 14:12 NKJV)

Jesus declared that we would do all of the works that He did, and even greater works. This is our spiritual inheritance in Christ. It is absolutely wonderful. This is His plan, His purpose, His desire. What we saw in the first generation of believers was a perfect reproduction of the Kingdom of God in men. Jesus was a wonderful teacher and minister who reproduced His life in His disciples.

When I first came to Christ it was through an encounter with the kingdom that was undeniable. One of the first problems that I had to face is that the church looks so different than it did in the first century. I couldn't see anything that fully measured up to the scriptures, which are supposed to be our source and norm for doctrine and teaching. I found things that came very close, but rarely did I see anything measure up to "all these and greater works." Yet after years of following Jesus, praying, studying the Scriptures, I have found that it is all clearly explained in His word. The simple truth is that all the life of Jesus was given to us when we were born again. It came into us as a seed, not fully grown. Think for a minute about an acorn. An acorn has the full potential of a forest of oak trees. Yet, in seed form it in no way resembles an oak tree, which it has the full potential to become. In the right context under the right conditions it will grow, and as it does it will more and more resemble a mature oak tree, but not until it is mature will it reproduce acorns. Only then does it have the ability to become a forest of oaks. The same pattern is seen all through nature. Think about it, the same thing is true of chicken eggs. They have the potential to become a living chicken, but as an egg there is no resemblance. The same thing is true of us. We have been born again of imperishable seed. We have been born again as children of God, but until we come to maturity we look nothing like Jesus, the pattern who we will become. It is in our DNA.

It is my passion and prayer that everything that is restricting the life of Christ in us from coming to maturity would be removed and that we all would come to the measure of the stature of the fullness of Christ. I praise Jesus that this will be the case before the end. There are two seeds growing in the earth and both will come to maturity. There is good news for the people of God, the bride will make herself ready. She will be a pure, spotless, and a glorious church!

The Gospel of Church

—⁓—

I like to preach the gospel of church. So much of Christianity today and many of the forms that have developed around it could be coined the gospel of individuals.

"That which was from the beginning, which we have heard, which we have seen with our eyes, which we have looked upon, and our hands have handled, concerning the Word of life— the life was manifested, and we have seen, and bear witness, and declare to you that eternal life which was with the Father and was manifested to us— that which we have seen and heard we declare to you, that you also may have fellowship with us; and truly our fellowship is with the Father and with His Son Jesus Christ. And these things we write to you that your joy may be full." (1 Jn 1:1-4 NKJV)

What John says here is absolutely amazing: the reason he preaches the gospel is so that people will have fellowship with the church. I would have expected that the reason he would declare everything he knew concerning "the Word of life" is so that people would believe in Jesus and have fellowship with Him. Actually, that is what he is saying but not how we may have expected. What John is telling his hearers is that if you have fellowship with the church, then you have fellowship with God the Father and Jesus Christ because that is who the church has fellowship with. Does that sound like the fellowship that you have in your church? It is exciting that this is God's desire for His church. There is even something else which is very terrible. John writes these things so that our joy may be full. Numerous times scriptures speak of our joy being full. For some strange reason I get the impression that God wants our joy to be full. It also seems to me that our joy being full is connected to communities of people called church where there is real fellowship with God and one another. Let us look at 1 John because it teaches us so much about the type of church god desires; it is one built around spiritual fellowship.

"This is the message which we have heard from Him and declare to you, that God is light and in Him is no darkness at all. If we say that we have fellowship with Him, and walk in darkness, we lie and do not practice the truth. But if we walk in the light as He is in the light, we have fellowship with one

another, and the blood of Jesus Christ His Son
cleanses us from all sin." (1 Jn 1:5-7 NKJV)

I think that people who want to quote 1 John
need to at least personally come to a conviction of
how to actually interpret the whole thing. Maybe we
will disagree, and that will be fine. Some of my best
growth has come from disagreements and usually
not the ones where I was right. When you quickly
read through 1 John, because of the way it is laid out
in English translations, it may appear like John says
that it is impossible for us to sin and then he turns
around and says that it is impossible for us not to sin.
Personally I do not believe John is confused and that
there is a very simple and easy way to understand
his epistle that makes sense and is edifying. I believe
in the perspicuity of scripture-not the perspicuity of
translations.

Look at some of the declarations:

- If we say we have fellowship with God and
  walk in darkness we are liars.
- There is no darkness in God and He has no
  fellowship with darkness.

I would challenge that many say they have fellowship with God but they actually only have fellowship
with forms of religion without power. There is no
presence of God in their life. Some people pretend
to have fellowship with God when they know that
they do not. I think that there are many people who
think they have fellowship with God but do not even

know what it really is. A tree is known by its fruits, and where there is true fellowship with God there are natural fruits of that fellowship. When these are lacking it is a sure sign that there is no fellowship with God.

If we walk in the light we have fellowship with one another and the blood of Jesus cleanses us from all of our sin. I have found is that in every country of the world, with every race, with every generation, with every social standing, when people walk in fellowship with God they have beautiful fellowship with one another. It doesn't mean that we all see eye to eye on everything, or that we are all perfect yet, but there is a beautiful love and fellowship. As a matter of fact, when we are in the Spirit we are being governed by love. Love cannot see faults; instead it covers them. It is in this context of fellowship with the Spirit of God and with one another that the blood of Jesus, or the life of Jesus, cleanses us of all sin. This is more than just forgiving us of our sin; it actually cleanses us of our sin. Jesus does more than forgive us of our sin, He saves us from it. Forgiveness of sin is the foundation and source for fellowship with His presence and for fellowship within His church. Fellowship is the context in which God cleanses us from our sin.

"If we say that we have no sin, we deceive ourselves, and the truth is not in us. If we confess our sins, He is faithful and just to forgive us our sins and to cleanse us from all unrighteousness. If we say that we have not

sinned, we make Him a liar, and His word is
not in us." (1 Jn 1:8-10 NKJV)

I would suggest that the context of 1 John is fellowship. This passage I believe refers to when fellowship
is broken. I do not believe that this is a general statement to be applied to all people at all times because
such an indictment doesn't fit the context of scripture.
It really makes a schizophrenic book. Essentially it
means that if we are out of fellowship with God (or
even the people of God) and we say that we have no
sin we deceive ourselves and the truth is not in us. It
is that simple. If we are out of fellowship, we have
broken the new covenant law, and we need to confess
our sin and repent. There are many ways to take the
confession of sin, but I have personally found that
if I can't pinpoint my sin I can't repent. Many times
we need to go to the Word, to prayer, and to brothers
and sisters until it is pinpointed. When the problem
is pinpointed and repented of, our fellowship is
restored. The sign of true repentance is not a restoration of a feeling of religious self-righteousness. The
sign that new covenant repentance has taken place is
restored fellowship.

If we are not having fellowship with light, then
we are having fellowship with darkness. Even if the
darkness appears like an angel of light dressed in
religious garb, it is fellowship with darkness unless
it bears the fruit of the Spirit. Every tree is known
by its fruit. The kingdom of God is in righteousness,
peace, and joy in the Holy Spirit. It causes people to
overflow with faith, hope and love. It is absolutely

invigorating. When that life is being quenched, be sure that there is fellowship somewhere with a lie and it needs to be repented of so that life can again flow freely.

Many times people spend much time repenting but never find a restoration of fellowship. I suggest that this is not new covenant repentance. There are so many things that Christians seem to do just to make themselves feel better religiously. For example, I am convinced that God is not glorified in the fact that we pray, but He is glorified in the answer to prayer. I am convinced that our joy is not full when we have prayed, but when we receive the answer to prayer. Yet so many times Christians create prayer lives and feel like they are very spiritual but never actually bear the fruit that God wants us to actually enjoy. They are actually being robbed of their inheritance in Christ. They are being tricked and deceived by the thief and robber and falling short of that which has been freely given us in Christ. I would much rather have my joy full.

For example, one time I was being robbed of the presence of God because I was worrying about money. I was in a place where I was serving the Lord, but it was very tight financially. At one point it was very hard to make ends meet (actually at more than one point): I remember going into a room at a local bible college where I liked to pray, and I prayed my heart out. I complained before God. Needless to say, the presence of God and the fruit of the kingdom were absent. I didn't realize it but I was having fellowship with a lie. After wasting a considerable amount of time praying, I finally remembered that Jesus told us that pagans sought after such things. We are not to worry about these things but rather to seek first the kingdom. I repented to God for my worry, my doubt and my unbelief and the wonderful peace that passes all understanding flooded my consciousness. Later that day someone who didn't know I had such a need put a significant sum of money in my hand. I learned a lot that day. Times of refreshing truly follow repentance.

The book of 1 John vigorously drives home the two-edged truth that first God will forgive us of our sins and then He will go beyond that and actually cleanse us from all unrighteousness. Maybe repetition is the mother of learning. God will forgive us and then cleanse us. Quit trying to cleanse yourself. Receive His forgiveness, and then He will cleanse you.

> "My little children, these things I write to you, so that you may not sin. And if anyone sins, we have an Advocate with the Father, Jesus Christ the righteous. And He Himself is the propitiation for our sins, and not for ours only but also for the whole world." (1 Jn 2:1-2 NKJV)

How can John say that he writes these things so that we may not sin and also maintain that everyone is sinning, and if we say otherwise we are liars? He is saying is that his desire is that we should walk in unbroken fellowship with God and one another, and if that fellowship is broken then we certainly have sinned and need to repent. If we find ourselves in that state then let us remember that we are forgiven because of Jesus. We have an advocate with the Father, Jesus Christ the righteous, who declares we are forgiven. Let us never lose sight that our forgiveness was fully accomplished at Calvary.

So often Christians go forth into the world and proclaim that God loves sinners. They boldly proclaim that it doesn't matter what you have done because Jesus died on the cross for your sins, and that if you will repent and believe you will be forgiven. Then, after they have become Christians, they act as though suddenly they no longer are welcome to come to God for forgiveness because they should have known better. This simply quenches life in the Spirit and makes Christianity unbearable. It leads to death of every sort.

We are called to develop Christian community or church in such a way where there is real fellowship with God and with one another. Community that is built upon forgiveness and love is the context where we will grow together into Him who is the head. Church is the context where people can come to maturity and be revealed as sons of God.

A Kingdom Potluck

—∿—

I have a hierarchy of desires in Christ. The first is to see people come to maturity. I have a passion to see the life of Christ reproduced in His people. It is the very same life that is in Jesus, and anything less simply will not do. We saw it wonderfully reproduced in the first generation apostles. My next desire is to see the church baptized with the Holy Spirit. That is because Holy Spirit baptism is God's ordained means to build up the church. Third, my desire is to see people born again. My desire for these things are probably equal, but the best way to see people born again is to see people come to maturity in Christ, and the best way for that to happen is for people who are born again to be baptized with the Holy Spirit so that they can grow into maturity.

When a child is born into this world, the home that he grows up in plays a very significant role in who that child will become. It can nurture that life into maturity, or it can restrict it in immaturity. The same thing is true with a baby Christian and the church. How do we develop a context where Christians can come to maturity? Certainly there are many important elements that must be in place in the church for Christians to grow to maturity, but I would like to look at one in particular that is incredibly important.

I am not a great mathematician, and I don't expect to ever be one. Yet I figured out a simple truth that makes mathematical sense to me. If I run hard after God and receive as much as I can by myself I will have severe limitations on how much I have. If I run hard after God with a group of others who are running hard after God, and we all take what we receive and hold it in common we will all be very rich and will grow very much. It is sort of like a Kingdom potluck.

> "He who receives you receives Me, and he who receives Me receives Him who sent Me. He who receives a prophet in the name of a prophet shall receive a prophet's reward. And he who receives a righteous man in the name of a righteous man shall receive a righteous man's reward. And whoever gives one of these little ones only a cup of cold water in the name of a disciple, assuredly, I say to you, he shall by no means lose his reward." (Mt 10:40-42 NKJV)

Every time that we receive the gift of God that is in another person we will receive the reward of that gift. Every time that we reject the gift of God in another we are robbed of the blessing that their gift would bring to us. So many times we are unable to receive the gift of God in others because it doesn't conform to the rules in our hidden manual of what we believe God's limits are. I'm telling you, if God can speak through an ass like He did with Balaam, then it sure gives me hope. So many times we stand before Jesus and proclaim "isn't this the carpenter's son?"

One of the things that I can't stand is how the prosperity gospel is often proclaimed. I believe poverty is part of the curse that is being dealt with by the blood of Jesus. I believe that sin at many various levels empowers the curse of poverty and that the gospel deals with them all. My problem is that many are approaching it from an angle that is simply out of bounds. Without realizing it, Christians often act in ways that are simply a form of pagan magic, expecting that rituals put God at your debt and that by them God is forced to act. So many times it is simply man trying to use God for their own agenda. Many times such things empower the carnal flesh that the gospel commands is to be put to death. I have seen things in Christianity that has made me ashamed. Ministers have sent me letters where they gave me a matrix that took how much debt we owed and told us to send a certain amount of money to their ministry. Then we were supposed to put the red stickers they gave us on all our bill stubs which read "paid in full." Supposedly the Lord told him to do this and that if people would obey they would be completely delivered from their debt. Such tactics are nothing more than a pagan ritual that empowers the carnal flesh and leads astray gullible people.

There was a time when I found the heavens like brass. I had my hands full of teaching tapes by many ministers but found them as satisfying as eating cardboard. The Lord dealt with me about spiritual pride. After I repented, the heavens opened up and the very same tapes that I thought were wretched ministered an incredible amount of life to me. I began to dig into many tapes and books. I was going to receive as much as I could no matter how earthen the vessel it came through. Around that time a name was brought to my attention who I always assumed taught much of the things like the ministry I mentioned above. Truthfully I had judged this guy and had never read one of his books or heard any of his preaching. To be quite honest, I really didn't know anything about him. I went and got some of his books, and they were a wealth of blessing to me.

Another time I found myself ministering with people who had caught the prosperity gospel "flu." I watched them take an offering, and it was very much the same ritual, yet the spirit of the Lord restrained me from acting. As I stood and watched I realized that the sincere intention of this minister was to see the people blessed. He really believed that if he got people to sow money into an offering that it would put God at their debt so their debts would be released. What he didn't see is that it still empowers people to be focused on something other than the Lord. The Lord gave me such compassion for them, but even more than that, those same people ministered incredible life to me in so many other areas. Just because we get it wrong on one thing, or even many things it doesn't mean we do not have anything of God to offer others. Can anything good come out of Nazareth? You bet it can.

> "For this reason we also thank God without ceasing, because when you received the word of God which you heard from us, you welcomed it not as the word of men, but as it is in truth, the word of God, which also effectively works in you who believe." (1 Th 2:13 NKJV)

Look at the effects of receiving the gift of God in one another. It causes thanksgiving without ceasing. Not a bad result. Look at the other side of the coin. It actually works effectively in those who received it. There is no way to get around it, so many are living in a spiritual wasteland because they are disconnected with life. They may believe in Jesus, but they are disconnected from His life among His people. Some of these people may even be going to church, but they are not connected to life. It is one of the most heart breaking realities under the sun that a person should go to church and not find the fullness of God.

I am convinced that the only way to truly grow in the Lord is to receive the Lord in His body. I believe that we need to develop churches where we are connected to one another in such a way that life is explosive rather than restricted. Let us take some instruction from the word.

"Now the multitude of those who believed were of one heart and one soul; neither did anyone say that any of the things he possessed was his own, but they had all things in common. And with great power the apostles gave witness to the resurrection of the Lord Jesus. And great grace was upon them all. Nor was there anyone among them who lacked; for all who were possessors of lands or houses sold them, and brought the proceeds of the things that were sold, and laid them at the apostles' feet; and they distributed to each as anyone had need." (Ac 4:32-35 NKJV)

First, we see that there was a multitude, and yet they were of one heart and soul. See the possibilities of the restrictions being removed in Christ. So much of the battle is to get our unity correct. There are so many false Christs. I know that people can develop unity around many innocuous things such as playing pool, supporting a sports team, watching birds, and even around a language that was created for a television show such as people have done with Star Trek. Even worse, people can develop unity around things that are sinful, such as around gossiping, criticism, intellectual pride, dead religion, clubbing, drugs, sexual immorality and the list could go on. The thing is, when our unity is built around fellowship in the Spirit, we find that unity creates abundance of life. All other unity will eventually destroy life. All divisions are removed, yet a beautiful diversity is able to develop. This is why true church can be cross-gener-ational, cross-racial, and also cross-social status. There is true unity only in Jesus Christ. I believe that true expressions of church will not be limited to a certain age, race, or social culture but will unify them in Christ. The greatest division in the world is destroyed in Christ: the division between Jew and gentile. Eventually it shall be manifested in history.

Next, no one said that anything that they possessed was their own; they held all things in common. While some misinformed Christians see this as a mandate for socialism, the real point is actually something completely different. Scripture clearly shows that early Christians personally possessed property, homes and other personal possessions. There is much in the New Testament that affirms personal property. The most important lesson from this passage show how those first generation Christians acted with their possessions. First, their willingness to sacrifice them for the good of the body is a beautiful expres-sion that in Christ we are actually born again into a new family. Second, the way they used their posses-sions demonstrates how, as a disciple, everything becomes subservient to the kingdom of God. There was no form or requirement in the early church that dictates that when someone became a Christian they sold everything they had and joined a commune. A natural fruit of true biblical spirituality is expressed in the church that whenever there was a need, whoever had the means to meet that need did so. When we are willing to sacrifice anything we possess to build up the people of God, it will cause no one to lack anything, and we will all be rich and prosper in Christ. When we hold all things in common, we all possess all things. This was the context that allowed the apostles to give testimony to the resurrection of Jesus with great power and for great grace to be upon them all. It is the context that allows people to grow very quickly because everyone is working together.

Because we were talking about math, maybe it would be good to put things into a mathematical equation. Because people in the body of Christ love to talk and teach so much about prosperity, let us call this....

The prosperity equation:

Receiving the gift of God in others + freely giving the gift of God in me to others= great riches and prosperity.

The middle part of the equation is that we would all freely give the gift of God that is in us to others. This is so important that it is actually what distinguishes those who are true sons of God from those who are false.

"Then the righteous will answer Him, saying, 'Lord, when did we see You hungry and feed You, or thirsty and give You drink? When did we see You a stranger and take You in, or naked and clothe You? Or when did we see You sick, or in prison, and come to You?' And the King will answer and say to them, 'Assuredly, I say to you, inasmuch as you did

it to one of the least of these My brethren,
you did it to Me.'" (Mt 25:37-40 NKJV)

When we are born again, the life of Jesus starts to
grow in us. His life was a living sacrifice, poured out
in love for others. Our lives should imitate that. One
of the major fruits of salvation is that we are saved
from being self-centered into being self-sacrificing
in love. Without this fruit in our life, we better make
sure we are born again. For example, if we often find
ourselves focused upon "what is in it for me" instead
of seeking how to serve God and others, then we
should examine ourselves carefully. This is worshipping self and not the Lord. This kind of Christianity
deceives some people into believing they are born
again when they are not and leaves true Christians
wandering in circles through the wilderness of spiritual immaturity. Self-centered religion causes church
to be a place where people go to feel good rather than
a place of self-sacrifice. God is going to destroy this
kind of religion before the end. It robs people from
coming to spiritual maturity.

The simple truth is that a good tree bears good
fruit, and a bad tree bears bad fruit. A tree is known
by its fruit. If we are not bearing good fruit we better
work out our salvation with fear and trembling. The
Kingdom of this world operates in such a way where
everyone is all about what is in it for them. The heart
of it puts self as God. It is seen in selfishness, self-
righteousness, and self-centeredness. It is a kingdom
ruled by fear and therefore seeks to protect itself. It
results in "I am blessed at your expense." It results

in darkness, death, and every form of curse. The kingdom of God is governed by love. It is demonstrated in ways such as: I will bless you, and in doing so I will be blessed. When everyone is giving everything in their power to be a blessing to others, everyone will be enriched and will lack nothing. Such a kingdom will destroy everything that robs people of life and will result in every kind of blessing, both natural and spiritual.

I cannot emphasize enough how important it is that we come to spiritual maturity. Spiritual maturity is being mature in love. Such mature love would have radical implications for society. For example, it would have an incredible impact on how we define success. What if we were to define success in how much of a blessing we can be to others? Think of the incredible social implications of such a simple thing. Yet the truth is that the letter of the law by itself reveals that we lack the power to actually walk in love. This is why only a good tree can bear good fruit. We need to make the tree good, and its fruit will be good as well. We need to be born again, but from there we need to grow to maturity so that we bear spiritual fruit. An immature tree bears no fruit.

The context for us to grow mature is through giving and receiving the gift of God that is in one another. We know that we love because He first loved us. We know that whoever is forgiven much the same will love much. We can only give what we have first received. All good things come from God, and He has freely given them to us in Christ. He is the source. Only when we have experienced His love will His love be reproduced in us so that people can actually experience God through us.

I will tell you the story of a lady who came into fellowship with a church where I was serving. She was going around to churches asking for prayer because her daughter was having an abortion. When she came into our meeting, we stopped what we were doing, and prayed for her. I do not know why, but my big mouth did what it is very adept at doing, which is getting me into unusual situations. I told her that I would do more than pray for her, I would go and speak with her daughter. Well, I went to her house several times, but because of the situation, her daughter was staying away from home. I found out where she worked and said that I would speak to her there. It was only when I was pacing outside of her workplace did the ridiculousness of the situation hit me. I was about to go into a place of business and try to talk someone out of having an abortion who had never met me before. Well, the grace of God is amazing. For some unknown reason, she decided to take a break and went outside to speak with a stranger who brought up a very difficult topic. Somehow God worked, and she kept her child!

A good bit of time went on and we didn't hear anything from the girl's mother. Then one day another member of the church was on his way to the prayer meeting and felt he should cut through the woods. There are train tracks that run through the woods where many people commit suicide. This area has one of the highest suicide rates in Europe. As he went through the woods, he found the woman's mother in the woods about to do commit suicide. He talked her out of it and brought her to church where she became a Christian. Praise Jesus! See how wonderfully God works through His body. I will refer to her as "the new Christian."

There is another particular person in our church who has an incredible gift. She really loves people! (Actually, there are many others who have the same gift in that church because it is in the DNA.) She meets people and thinks they are wonderful. She sees them from eyes that are blinded by God's love. I have watched this person love types of people who have been rejected by others their whole life. It is easy to love people who love us, but the real test of God's love in our life is to love those who are difficult to love. I have seen her love people who make loving them a challenge. Before long, God's love for them that is expressed through her delivers them from darkness and empowers the life of Christ in them. It reproduces the same love. I will refer to her as "my friend."

The new Christian would spend a lot of time at my friend's house, and she was really blessed by going there. Then one day as this new Christian was visiting my friend's house she began throwing things in a fit of anger. There were substances and circumstances that had enhanced her mood. Because of this outburst, this new Christian quit visiting my friend's house because she understandably thought she would not be welcome. (She avoided relationship just like Adam and Eve did when they saw they were naked and therefore ashamed.) After several months went by, my friend ran into the new Christian in the grocery store.

"It is really good to see you. Where have you been? I've really missed you," my friend said.

"I thought I wouldn't be welcome any more after what I did," the new Christian replied.

"That's nonsense. You are always welcome. It is like you are a part of our family."

That day the life of Christ was gloriously revealed through one of His children. Within the proper context, new Christians will grow up and reveal the life of Christ in every way. Later this new Christian went to visit her brother with one of her other brothers. The brother she went to visit drank and became abusive. She responded with the very same grace and love as she had received, and her other brother asked "how can you be so gracious?"

She could have honestly said that God had treated her with that type of love through one of His Children. God's love becomes manifested in the flesh as the life of Jesus is reproduced in God's sons.

The point is, that when we all give and receive the life of God that is in one another, we will grow up very fast. There is so much that is true in the life of Christ, and it is already in the new DNA we received when we were born again. We just need the right context for it to grow to maturity and show itself. The way that we grow is this: as we see Him we become like Him. One of the best ways for us to see Him is to receive Him through His people who know Him in ways that we do not already know him.

For this to become a reality, we need people to freely give what God has given them.

"Will a man rob God? Yet you have robbed Me! But you say, 'In what way have we robbed You?' In tithes and offerings. You are cursed with a curse, For you have robbed Me, Even this whole nation." (Mal 3:8-9 NKJV)

Certainly this is a very specific scripture referring to a very specific situation which has many different applications. There is one particular principle that is very true. When we rob God of our tithes and offerings, it certainly will result in a curse. We have gifts that are meant to be used to build up God's house and when they aren't brought into the house of God people are robbed of that gift. What greater curse can there be than to be robbed of the Life of Christ. In Christ we are called to offer our whole lives as a living sacrifice. We are called to serve one another in love and when we withhold this from the body of Christ we are robbing God's house. From one perspective we are robbing other people of the grace of God that is meant to be ministered through us and from another perspective we are robbing God of His inheritance in His saints.

There is an incredible dignity and responsibility that God invests in all of His Children. Every Christian has an equal responsibility to fulfill the great commission, and every Christian has a ministry to fulfill to this end. I remember when the Lord gave me a number of teachings to help release people into their ministries, and then He gave me a surprising dream that prepared me for trials. I was preaching in a room filled with people about how every Christian has an equal responsibility to fulfill the great commission. I was excited because of the explosive growth I knew it would cause when people engaged in their ministries. The result that I got was that a good number of people stood up and started speaking against what I was saying. The reality is that they didn't want to touch the responsibility and wanted to keep forms and doctrines that allowed them to feel comfortable shirking from their responsibility. While I was hearing everything they were saying I could see how to destroy their arguments with the Word of God, but an angel came and stopped me and told me that I had proclaimed the word I was meant to proclaim and that those who had ears to hear would hear.

When we build churches where people are free to grow in the anointing and ministry that God has given them we will see explosive growth. I do not believe in democratic churches. God still anoints and works through leaders. There is a difference between mature and immature, between gifts and callings, but the point is that true spiritual leadership will develop a context where people are free to grow in Christ and will be able to protect that life as well. So many people want to be told what to do, and so many leaders want to tell people what to do, but this will always result in restricted life. So many desire cookie cutter Christianity, but such religion is quite dead and boring to me. We need to learn how to release the ministry that God has entrusted to His people, and we need to thank God that He hasn't called us to do it all. I remember someone upset at me because I wasn't doing certain things that they expected me to do. I told them I wasn't going to do it, and I wasn't going to feel bad about it either. We are a body. There are people with gifts, anointings and callings that I don't have. Not only will they be able to do things that I can't do, but they will see things that I will never see. There is no point trying to do it all. Praise Jesus He has put us in His body. So many people get frustrated because they see things lacking in a church. What a surprise! They don't realize that if they see a problem they have a responsibility to do something about it other than complaining and backbiting.

People can go to church their whole lives and never engage the work of the Lord. Not only can they go to church their whole lives, but they can be involved in all kinds of church activities and planned ministries and never engage in the work the Lord called them to. As long as we are always doing something other than what God has called and anointed us to do we are simply playing games and not engaging in our Daddy's kingdom business. This is robbing the house of God. Every Christian has so much value that for them to not bring their lives into the service of the Kingdom of God is actually robbery.

Look at some scriptures that speak of such things.

"There are diversities of gifts, but the same Spirit. There are differences of ministries, but the same Lord. And there are diversities of activities, but it is the same God who works all in all. But the manifestation of the Spirit is given to each one for the profit of all:" (1 Co 12:4-7 NKJV)

This little verse is absolutely beautiful. The manifestation of the Spirit is given to each Christian for the profit of all. Every Christian is meant to have a manifestation of the Spirit and that manifestation is the very tool for enriching others. The gifts of the Spirit are God's ordained means for building up the church. If we try to build it up any other way we are simply wasting time.

One of the first pastors that I had was Ted Junkuntz. He has been kicked out of fellowship from numerous denominations because he is unwilling to compromise the Word of God as he sees it. One of the things that started the whole process was writing an article about the gifts of the spirit that declared that they are not optional extras for the church. Such a simple and obvious biblical statement can cause all kinds of trouble. Many people would ask why something so obvious would be so controversial. The simple truth is that when people have sincerely invested many years of their lives in a system they do not want to have to face the fact that what they have built is crooked.

When I first became a Christian my Grandma gave me many tapes of preaching she had collected over the years. There were many teachings that were a blessing to me, but my favorites were the ones from Bob Mumford. He could say something in such a funny way that you never forgot it. He had one teaching on Amos and the Plumb line where he brought out a poignant fact. Many times people are busy building away and then God sends a prophet. The prophet comes along and puts a plumb line to the work and reveals that the building is crooked. The people have two options, either fix the building or kill the prophet. Well, it is much easier to kill the prophet.

The house of God must be built exactly as God designed it, or it will eventually have to be torn down and rebuilt. God's design is for the church to be built through the gifts of the Spirit. Every Christian has been given spiritual gifts for the purpose of building God's house. If anyone fails to minister in the gift God has called them to minister in, then everyone is robbed. If we labor our little tails off, but not according to the spiritual gift God has given us, then everyone is still robbed. People who try to build the church with the flesh will eventually burn out, but people who build by the spirit never will. People who build by the flesh are not building authentic church, and it will eventually have to be torn down and rebuilt.

> "...but, speaking the truth in love, may grow up in all things into Him who is the head — Christ — from whom the whole body, joined and knit together by what every joint supplies, according to the effective working by which every part does its share, causes growth of the body for the edifying of itself in love." (Eph 4:15-16 NKJV)

This passage comes directly after a discussion about how everyone has a measure of grace given to them, then about the fivefold ministry which culminates in the church coming to the measure of the stature of the fullness of Christ. It teaches that we will grow up into Him who is the head, who is Christ. This growth or edifying of the body (building itself up) happens when every member does their share. It is that simple. If the people of God are being restricted from fulfilling the ministry God has given them, then the body will never come to maturity. If people are unwilling to do their part, the body will never come to maturity. If people do not receive the ministry of every member, then the body will never come to maturity. If we develop church where every member engages the spiritual ministry that God has called them to we will see explosive growth.

The final part of the prosperity equation is that all these things will cause us to be rich and prosperous. We will come to the measure of the stature of the fullness of Christ. We will come to a perfect man. We will lack nothing. We will literally see the manifestation of the kingdom of God at hands length, or rather here now.

We see an example of this in David and Solomon's reign.

"All King Solomon's drinking vessels were gold, and all the vessels of the House of the Forest of Lebanon were pure gold. Not one was silver, for this was accounted as nothing in the days of Solomon. For the king had merchant ships at sea with the fleet of Hiram. Once every three years the merchant ships came bringing gold, silver, ivory, apes, and monkeys. So King Solomon surpassed all the kings of the earth in riches and wisdom." (1 Ki 10:21-23 NKJV)

Despite how wonderful this was, it still falls short of the glory of God. It is only a shadow of what is available in the new covenant. The glory of the old covenant had to fade. It actually died the day Jesus declared "it is finished." In its death it has brought forth much fruit. There is now a kingdom whose glory will never fade. Just as the old covenant came to a climax, so will the new covenant. That is where we are moving towards in history. That is what was prophesied in many of the scriptures we have looked at. That is what we are called to be a part of now.

Rebuilding the Temple

—⟋⟍—

"Now, therefore, you are no longer strangers and foreigners, but fellow citizens with the saints and members of the household of God, having been built on the foundation of the apostles and prophets, Jesus Christ Himself being the chief corner*stone,* in whom the whole building, being fitted together, grows into a holy temple in the Lord, in whom you also are being built together for a dwelling place of God in the Spirit." (Eph 2:19-22 NKJV)

God is building His Christian temple in the midst of the earth right now. It will be His dwelling place. He will manifest His name there, which means He will demonstrate who He is. His glory will be manifested just like it was in the first Christian temple; just like it was in Jesus. We need to get the blueprints of the temple and build it exactly as God designed. The blueprints are all in scripture. One particular story in scripture teaches us much about building the temple. It is the story of rebuilding the old covenant temple through Zerubabbel and Joshua.

Because of their sin, the Jew's kingdom was overthrown and their temple was destroyed in 586BC by the Babylonians. While in captivity, the prophet Daniel discerned through the scriptures that God had appointed that He would restore them in 70 years to Jerusalem. When the appointed time came, a decree went forth from Cyrus (the ruler of the Persians who conquered the Babylonians) that the Jews were to return and rebuild the temple at Jerusalem. A group of people returned to Jerusalem to rebuild the temple. They set up the altar, and sacrifices were reinstated. They returned to Jerusalem with a commission to rebuild the temple, but the rebuilding actually stopped. After construction on the temple had ceased for about 14 years, God sent the prophet Haggai to turn the hearts of the Jews back to the work they were called to do.

During the old covenant, the temple was the place where God dwelt. The reason that the temple in Haggai's day was in ruins was due to the Jew's sins against the old covenant. Their sin caused God to depart from the temple, and with His presence gone, the city was ruined. If the Jews would have been faithful to the covenant their kingdom could have remained intact. Because of their disobedience their kingdom was removed from the earth. Today God is looking to rebuild His temple and manifest his kingdom on earth. The church, like the Jews of Haggai's day, has been in a Babylonian captivity.

Zerubbabel was the governor in Jerusalem who was responsible for rebuilding the temple. Zerubbabel's name means "born in Babylon," and that is where he was born. Christianity today has been born in Babylon. We have grown up in a church that often operates in the ways of Babylon rather than the ways of God. We have an inheritance in the Kingdom of God that God is restoring right now. He is building His temple and His kingdom will be manifested in the world.

Why did the rebuilding cease? After all, it was the revivalists who returned to Jerusalem for the very purpose of rebuilding the temple. I am sure that these people had imaginations of what to expect. It was a time of revival. I am sure they dreamed of glory and blessing, of streets paved with gold. They seemed to have favor all around from God and men. They were the ones who responded to God's call. They were the real deal. After all, the majority of the captives actually decided to remain in captivity. They had already set down roots, had financial security, they had developed a pretty good standard of living there in captivity. Everyone knows that it is tough to start over. I can almost hear the revivalist on their way back to Jerusalem talking about how sad it is that so many people loved the world more than kingdom and therefore remained in captivity. Little did they know how much the captivity had gotten into them.

When they got home they set up the sacrifices and began to rebuild the temple. Then visitors showed up. The Samaritans came and asked to help with the rebuilding. Here the Jews were presented with an opportunity to compromise. Many hands would make the work light, but these revivalists knew better. After all, the whole reason for being in captivity was compromising the Word of God. Because their help was rejected the Samaritans became enemies of the work and very diligent enemies at that. Soon the Jews were forced by armed men to stop rebuilding the temple. They should have continued the work on the temple despite opposition. God would have defended the work. If they had known the scriptures, they would have expected severe opposition to what they were doing. They would have expected God to take care of it also. They were restoring the temple of God, and the kingdom of darkness would do anything to stop it. If people would trust in the Lord He would stop their enemies. The people were probably tired of the warfare which I guarantee was much more than the physical opposition. They probably were looking for an excuse to quit. The whole thing probably wasn't turning out how they expected. When they returned as the zealous revivalists, they thought they were taking Easy Street and ended up on Perseverance Blvd.

We too need to persevere like the Jews did. I remember Stephanie telling me once, "The idea of living by faith and reality of it are two very different things." Even when our expectations are shattered we must persevere in obedience to the Lord. The Jews decided to obey the devil and quit the work on the temple. This brings us to a place where for fourteen years the work of the Lord was being neglected.

""""Thus speaks the Lord of hosts, saying: 'This people says, "The time has not come, the time that the Lord's house should be built."""" Then the word of the Lord came by Haggai the prophet, saying, "Is it time for you yourselves to dwell in your paneled houses, and this temple to lie in ruins?" Now therefore, thus says the Lord of hosts: "Consider your ways! "You have sown much, and bring in little; You eat, but do not have enough; You drink, but you are not filled with drink; You clothe yourselves, but no one is warm; And he who earns wages, Earns wages to put into a bag with holes." Thus says the Lord of hosts: "Consider your ways! Go up to the mountains and bring wood and build the temple, that I may take pleasure in it and be glorified," says the Lord." (Hag 1:2-8 NKJV)

Not only have the people quit the work the Lord, but they actually build their own theology to justify their actions. They used scriptures to help them feel secure in their disobedience.

"For the time will come when they will not endure sound doctrine, but according to their own desires, *because* they have itching ears, they will heap up for themselves teachers; and they will turn *their* ears away from the truth, and be turned aside to fables." (2 Ti 4:3-4 NKJV)

These people wanted an excuse to disobey the will of God. I can almost picture them pulling out the Word and showing that although the prophesy was for 70 years of captivity, because the temple was destroyed after they officially went into captivity, the 70 years was not up yet for the temple. It is dangerous when people build their theology to fit their experience rather than let their theology become the source and norm for their experience.

Look at how convenient this is, the house of God is in ruins while everyone is very diligently laboring to build their own house! Oh the tragedy of this. Today many people are busy building their own house while the house of God is in ruins. Many people are so concerned about their own agenda that they have no time for the Lord's agenda, yet most of them probably do not realize it. The Jews believed the doctrines of seducing spirits which were saying that the time was not yet for rebuilding the house. And why not? They were used to the religion of captivity which adapted itself to the fact that there was no temple even though it left the world with no expression of the kingdom of God on earth. I bet that many were content with their personal relationship with God. I bet many were satisfied with the forms of religion that developed out of captivity. Today, the church rarely looks like the pattern set forth in scripture, but so many are content because they know they have believed in Jesus as their Lord and savior and they will go to heaven when they die. People have become content with forms of religion that are devoid of power, and even worse they have built bastions of theology to keep them secure and at ease. Every once in a while there is a breakout of the kingdom of God, but all too often people become disillusioned because they do not realize that such a thing puts them on hell's top 100 hit list so they give up the work. We must never forget that how we end the race is much more important than how we start.

> "If you endure chastening, God deals with you as with sons; for what son is there whom a father does not chasten? But if you are without chastening, of which all have become partakers, then you are illegitimate and not sons." (Heb 12:7-8 NKJV)

All who are legitimate children of God will be disciplined. No one likes discipline when they are going through it, but later they are very grateful that God didn't write them off. These Jews who were so busy trying to build their own houses find the Lord God almighty is purposely frustrating them. They are laboring hard for nothing because they are not obeying the voice of God. Finally when they are at a place where they are willing to listen, God sends His prophet Haggai who points out what they can no longer deny. God is frustrating their labors and will continue to do so until they repent and do what He called them to do: to rebuild the temple. Praise Jesus, they obey and begin rebuilding the temple.

Then another prophesy comes that contrasts the state of disobedience and obedience.

"Then Haggai answered and said, '"So is this people, and so is this nation before Me,' says the Lord, 'and so is every work of their hands; and what they offer there is unclean.'" (Hag 2:14 NKJV)

This is the end of a prophetic prelude to a promise. He is here reminding them of where they were before they began rebuilding the house. He wants the lesson to be burned into their consciousness so that they always seek to keep their hearts right with God.

Right before this verse Haggai actually goes to the priests and asks them about ceremonial law in order to teach them a simple truth. If someone is carrying something that is holy and it touches something unclean, that which is unclean is not made holy because it touches something holy. On the other hand if something unclean touches something clean that which is clean is made unclean. Just bring kids who have been playing in the mud into a nice clean house and see what happens. That clean house will make the kids clean. Seriously, the point is that if we are disobeying the Lord in one area it makes everything unclean. We may do many things right, just like those who returned from captivity and set up sacrifices; because they quit rebuilding the temple it made their sacrifices unclean. There is no point trying to pretend that we are pleasing God when we are walking in disobedience. There is no point calling Jesus Lord and not doing what He commands. You can't pull that one over on God. These people were doing many right things, but the fact they were obsessed with building their own homes while the house of God was in ruins made it all unclean.

God in His rich mercy contended with those who in disobedience were building their homes while the house of God was in ruins. So many times we have a silly notion that anything that rocks the boat can't be from God. Let me just say that God is always rocking the boat. He loves us so much that He will not let us continue to compromise His Word forever. Many times the Prince of Peace shows up in our lives with a two-edged sword. I know He has shown up that way in my life many times and I am very grateful that He does. Often when God shows up to rock the boat, He does it through one of His servants. Such people will actually be trying to bring people into peace with God and will be labeled a peace wrecker when in truth they are a peace maker. Sometimes our idol of Christian unity is nothing more than a disguise for compromising the Word of God. If we don't repent, and we are legitimate Children, we can expect a spanking. I pray that I would obey discipline while He is still gently reprimanding rather than having to wait until He has to actually give me a whooping. Unfortunately that has not always been my history. The fear of the Lord is the beginning of wisdom, and sometimes it begins with a red bottom. These people had a red bottom because they weren't rebuilding the house of God. They repented and obeyed the will of God at the preaching of Haggai. A blessing is proclaimed over them because of their obedience.

"'And now, carefully consider from this day
forward: from before stone was laid upon
stone in the temple of the Lord— since those
days, when one came to a heap of twenty
ephahs, there were but ten; when one came to
the wine vat to draw out fifty baths from the
press, there were but twenty. I struck you with
blight and mildew and hail in all the labors
of your hands; yet you did not turn to Me,'
says the Lord. 'Consider now from this day
forward, from the twenty-fourth day of the
ninth month, from the day that the foundation of the Lord's temple was laid—consider
it: Is the seed still in the barn? As yet the vine,
the fig tree, the pomegranate, and the olive
tree have not yielded fruit. But from this day
I will bless you.'"" (Hag 2:15-19 NKJV)

This is the most wonderful promise. God is basically saying, "Because you are building my house, I
will build yours." I would much rather have a house
that God built for me than one I built for myself.
When we seek first the Kingdom of God and His righteousness all of the things we need will be taken care
of. Even more than this, when God has commanded
us to be blessed, God's blessings will go far beyond
what we simply need.

The prophetic anointing often frustrates the
works of the enemy. During the time of Elisha, the
king of Syria was convinced that someone from
among his people was a traitor because the King of
Israel knew every trap that the king of Syria set. It

turns out it was just the prophet of God. The enemy is frustrated when the people of God receive a prophet because they receive the reward the prophet brings. Looking at the small remnant who are rebuilding the temple we see a group of people whose situation seems impossible. It *appears* that because they have given themselves to rebuilding the house of God their houses will be ruined. There is no seed in the barn and nothing has born any fruit. The future looks bleak. The pressure to take care of seemingly urgent needs instead of rebuilding the house of God is great. The prophetic anointing gets ahead of this and says, "Hold the course. Despite all appearances the Word of the Lord has proclaimed blessing, and you shall be blessed because of your obedience to the Lord."

Many times the battle people have to fight is over faith in God's Word against all the appearances of their circumstances. We have to look to those things that are unseen rather than what is seen and call those things that are not as though they are. Abraham was a great hero of faith, and He often looked very ridiculous. He leaves all of his family and people, all of his security because "God told him to." He runs around proclaiming "God is going to bless me," and in the natural made choices which according to the wisdom of the world would produce the very opposite of blessing. In a similar way, Elijah, in obedience and faith he does the very opposite thing you would expect. He soaked everything he wanted to catch on fire with water! The wisdom of God is foolishness to those who are perishing.

God told Abraham that his descendants will be as numerous as the sand on the shore or the stars of the sky. Doesn't He realize how old he and his wife are? I can imagine what people thought of him. One day he declares that all the males in his house were to be circumcised as a sign of the promises of God to him. There were probably many servants that he expected to be circumcised. Long after Abraham declares God's promise to him, Sarah remained barren. When all seemed impossible that she should have a son, she had a son. Fast forward. Abraham is about to sacrifice the lad, and Hebrews tells us that He still believed that through Isaac his descendants would proceed even if God had to raise him from the dead. He also believed that the Promised Land was his possession and died only owning a grave plot. He believed God despite all of his circumstances and any other voice to the contrary. In the end, God made good on His word.

Look at Moses. To all of the people who perished in the wilderness he seemed like a false prophet. He said that God would bring them in to the Promised Land and most of them died without seeing it. Yet God made good on His Word.

Here God promises that despite all outward appearances they will be blessed. God will bless them because they were obeying his will and rebuilding His house. There are so many times that we will find the same principle at work in our life. God will bless us when we obey His will. So many Christians are trying to build their own house and looking for God to bless them. They want a real blessing but are disqualified by their disobedience. If we will take care of God's business, He will take care of ours!

The prophetic anointing is very important for us as we seek to rebuild the temple of the Lord in this day. There is such warfare against the work of God that we need the prophetic anointing to keep the truth of God's Word before us rather than the appearance of circumstances. We need to rebuild the house of God so every member does his/her part. We need to see the Temple come to completion. We need to labor to see every Christian come to maturity. Let us look more at how the prophetic anointing was working when Zerubbabel and Joshua rebuilt the temple.

> "'Who is left among you who saw this temple in its former glory? And how do you see it now? In comparison with it, is this not in your eyes as nothing? Yet now be strong, Zerubbabel,' says the Lord; 'and be strong, Joshua, son of Jehozadak, the high priest; and be strong, all you people of the land,' says the Lord, 'and work; for I am with you,' says the Lord of hosts. 'According to the word that I covenanted with you when you came out of Egypt, so My Spirit remains among you; do not fear!' "For thus says the Lord of hosts: 'Once more (it is a little while) I will shake heaven and earth, the sea and dry land; and I will shake all nations, and they shall come to the Desire of All Nations, and I will fill this temple with glory,' says the Lord of hosts. 'The silver is Mine, and the gold is Mine,'

says the Lord of hosts. 'The glory of this latter
temple shall be greater than the former,' says
the Lord of hosts. 'And in this place I will
give peace,' says the Lord of hosts.'"" (Hag
2:3-9 NKJV)

There was incredible pressure for people to be
discouraged. They were surrounded by enemies all
around who would love to see them fail. All of the
glory that was once the Kingdom of Israel, especially under David and Solomon, was now only a
story. There were some who remembered the temple
of Solomon with the glory of God, the Ark, the Holy
fire, and the size and splendor of the building. In
their eyes, the rebuilt temple was insignificant in
every way. If they would have allowed it, discouragement would have destroyed what God was doing.
They were a very small group of people surrounded
by enemies and living under foreign rule. Even their
glorious temple didn't seem so glorious. It would
be easy to be disheartened and to give up but the
prophetic anointing comes and gives God's perspective on things, and it is a wonderful perspective
indeed.

First, the Lord is with them. He is with them just
like He was when Israel came out of Egypt. Therefore
they were not to be afraid despite the pressures they
are under. They were called to be strong despite the
appearance of their current situation. They looked like
Noah building the ark. It looked absolutely foolish.
They may have felt like the 10 unbelievers who spied
out the Promised Land and discouraged the people

declaring that Israel in the Promised Land would be like grasshoppers in a land of giants. But there was something God wanted them to know; the Lord is going to shake heaven and earth, all of their enemies will be overthrown, and the glory of this seemingly insignificant temple is going to supersede the glory of Solomon's temple.

When people set themselves to serve the Lord with all their heart, there will be all kinds of warfare. It is very common for people to become discouraged when that which God has called them to seems insignificant in the face of apparent circumstances. The same thing was true with the kingdom of Saul and David. Saul was the reigning king, but David was anointed to be king. Saul became the enemy of David because the Lord was with him. He had all the institutions, all the prestige and it appeared that anyone who allied himself with Saul had great opportunities for blessing and promotion. By all appearances you would want to ally yourself with him.

David on the other hand was hiding in caves. His mighty men were a rag tag group of outcasts; nothing spectacular. He had nothing apparent to offer people. He and his ragtag army had to leave Israel because it was too dangerous. At one point David even played a madman; foaming at his mouth to save his neck. Even David's mighty army of outcasts once wanted to kill him because an enemy came and looted their homes and family. It seemed that David only had trials and tribulations to offer. Except for one thing: God is with him! Besides Samuel, no one understood it and rejoiced over this truth more than Jonathan,

Saul's son. The problem is that when God had David
and his army out in the wilderness to prepare them
to enter into their inheritance, Jonathan was still in
the house of Saul. He never came out, and therefore
he perished with Saul when God gave the kingdom
to David.

No matter how insignificant it may seem, no
matter how despised by the world and ridiculed by the
institutions, I want to be identified with whatever and
whomever God identifies Himself with. All the treasures of Egypt are dung compared to the excellence
of being among the people of God in the presence of
Christ. Right now we are in a similar changing of the
order. We have been ever since Pentecost. Babylon,
the system of darkness which the kingdom of the
world is built upon will be destroyed.

The Kingdom of God is coming forth into its
own. It started like a mustard seed, but it is growing
and will come to maturity.

> "And again the word of the Lord came to
> Haggai on the twenty-fourth day of the month,
> saying, "Speak to Zerubbabel, governor of
> Judah, saying: 'I will shake heaven and earth.
> I will overthrow the throne of kingdoms; I will
> destroy the strength of the Gentile kingdoms.
> I will overthrow the chariots And those who
> ride in them; The horses and their riders shall
> come down, Every one by the sword of his
> brother. 'In that day,' says the Lord of hosts,
> 'I will take you, Zerubbabel My servant, the
> son of Shealtiel,' says the Lord, 'and will

make you like a signet ring; for I have chosen you,' says the Lord of hosts." (Hag 2:20-23 NKJV)

Again we see a prophetic encouragement. Again it could seem like this little group of people are like grasshoppers in a land of Giants but the Word of the Lord has spoken something better. The gentile kingdoms shall be overthrown and the Kingdom of God shall be firmly established. In that day, Zerubbabel will be like a signet ring. He will act as an ambassador of the Kingdom of God and will demonstrate kingdom authority.

The name Zerubbabel means born in Babylon. There are a people who are born in Babylon who are rebuilding the house of God in the midst of fierce enemies against all odds. When it is complete they will manifest kingdom authority as ambassadors of Christ.

Just like Haggai, Zechariah is filled with powerful teaching for this hour. I just want to look at one passage.

"Then the angel who talked with me answered and said to me, "Do you not know what these are?" And I said, "No, my lord." So he answered and said to me: "This is the word of the Lord to Zerubbabel: 'Not by might nor by power, but by My Spirit,' Says the Lord of hosts. 'Who are you, O great mountain? Before Zerubbabel you shall become a plain! And he shall bring forth the capstone With shouts of "Grace, grace to it!"'"'" Moreover the word of the Lord came to me, saying: "The hands of Zerubbabel Have laid the foundation of this temple; His hands shall also finish it. Then you will know That the Lord of hosts has sent Me to you." (Zec 4:5-9 NKJV)

This word actually came to pass with the temple that was rebuilt by Zerubbabel, but it also has a powerful prophetic significance for us today. First, not by power or might but by the Spirit of the Lord will this happen. The temple will be rebuilt God's ways, not Babylon's ways. It will be built by the power of the Spirit and not the strength of the flesh. The "great mountain" is every power structure of Babylon; it shall be destroyed by the power of God. It will not be able to stand. The temple that began to be built by those who were born in Babylon will certainly be built. The temple of the Lord, the body of Christ, shall be complete; we will come to spiritual maturity.

The book of Zachariah includes a call to all who remained in Babylon when the remnant returned to rebuild the temple. Once the temple is rebuilt, the authority of the kingdom of God will be manifested and destruction will come to Babylon. A prophetic call goes to those who remained in Babylon that they need to come out because Babylon is going to be destroyed. If the people of God do not come out of her they will be destroyed with her.

Jesus wouldn't have taught us to pray "Your kingdom come and Your will be done on earth as in heaven" if He didn't intend for it to actually happen. It is actually happening. I want to encourage everyone who is laboring for the church to come forth in maturity that it is guaranteed in the Word. I also want to encourage everyone that the kingdom strategy is not to try to argue and dialogue with those who are committed to remaining in Babylon. We need to rebuild the temple and invest our time and energy there. When the authority of the Kingdom of heaven is manifested many will actually return to Jerusalem. She will grow so much that she will be a city without walls with the glory of God in her midst. The true manifestation of kingdom life cannot be contained. It will reproduce.

Climbing a Mountain

—ɷ—

"And He Himself gave some to be apostles, some prophets, some evangelists, and some pastors and teachers, for the equipping of the saints for the work of ministry, for the edifying of the body of Christ, till we all come to the unity of the faith and of the knowledge of the Son of God, to a perfect man, to the measure of the stature of the fullness of Christ;" (Eph 4:11-13 NKJV)

In a very real way Christianity is best when it is like a relay race. The end of the race is the completed temple of God and the revelation of the sons of God who are conformed to the image of Christ. Unfortunately many people try to run by themselves. Those who don't treat it like a relay race force others to repeat the same part of the race.

I love white water rafting. I remember the first time I went white water rafting when I was a teenager in Boy Scouts. I was in the boat with a bunch of healthy athletic guys. We thought we were the stuff. We paddled with all of our might. I remember sticking my paddle in the water and pulling it through the water with all that I was worth. I looked over and saw that everyone else was doing the same. We were wildly screaming. In our minds we were the best, but we had nothing to compare ourselves to. Then, out of nowhere came a raft with young girls. They were younger and much smaller than us, yet they passed us like we were not moving at all. Even worse, it appeared that they were doing it effortlessly! Now we had a reference point for comparison. I stopped and thought about it and realized that there must be something we were missing. We decided to try to make our aim working together (as we were instructed to do originally) and everyone made it their goal to be in perfect unity with the lead rower while listening to the directions of the guide in back. We started moving at a much faster rate, and we were barely expending any energy.

There is so much that I learned from that simple experience. First, it took seeing it done right to show us what we were doing wrong. Only then did we stop doing it incorrectly. This is repentance; a change of mind that results in a change of direction. Many of us need to quit judging things by the values of the world or popular Christianity and let the Word of God be the standard by which we judge ourselves. Rather than letting it condemn us for the fact that we are rowing really hard yet hardly moving, we should let it inspire us that there is incredible spiritual power that we are called to actually experience.

Next we need to realize that Christianity is a team sport. As the Word has made clear, it is only when every member does their part that it causes growth. It is impossible to be walking in obedience to Christ and to be out of fellowship with the church. I say that boldly, and yet I am referring to God's definition of Church in the Word. So many times people have left fellowship with churches, but in reality they were never actually engaged in legitimate church, just forms of religion with no power. So many times people have gotten closer to the kingdom when they have gotten off the spiritual treadmill and left the systems that are designed to keep them in immaturity. Even if we have been hurt by churches and religious systems, we have been given a responsibility from Jesus Himself to be committed to legitimate church. We also have a responsibility to let nothing but love and compassion grow in our hearts for people who are stuck in limiting religious systems. So many times when people have been burned out by churches they "catch the flu." They end up catching bugs such as bitterness, frustration, disillusionment or other deadly "diseases." I have seen many people stay away from church because they were wronged. Instead of leaving the burden at the cross they carry it with them. The longer they carry it the more it destroys them.

Something else that is heartbreaking is that many of the religious systems that actually end up restricting people from coming to maturity have a measure of real life. I have seen it many times. People will run in the Spirit and get a hold of truth that results in real spiritual life, but then as time passes and the Spirit seeks to lead them into all truth, He can't get them to budge because they have built great kingdoms around the truth they already received. Such people often become unwilling to continue to grow. Because many are legitimate children of God, He begins striving with them to get them to be led by the Spirit again. The process often pierces them through with many sorrows and some begin to follow the Lord again. Unfortunately many others continue to stay in the rut and become hurt and bitter. Even some of the people who have moved out again can also become bitter towards the system they left, and bitterness always leads to bondage. The good news is that God is greater than all of the sin and failures of men. He is leading His church to become what He intended it to be from the beginning. All of the tribulations and sufferings of men are counted as well worth it when we experience the kingdom of God. The kingdom of God is a kingdom of men in unity with heaven. Therefore they are in unity with God and one another.

There is incredible power and life where there is unity in the Spirit. God desires such unity for all of His children. I am very careful to add the word Spirit because every group has unity around something. When we are growing in the grace and knowledge of God, problems can arise that disrupt the unity we were experiencing. These are labor pains which give birth to new life. Many are afraid of conflict or crisis that are often the very birth pains of life. One of the ministries I was involved with was experiencing a lot of success at one point. People of several churches asked why it was so successful when they could hardly get people to come to their own church. The answer was simple: we had unity in the Spirit. After some time the Spirit started to burden us in ways that called us to deeper things than we were already experiencing. I remember how some of the key people in the team who were relied upon the most eventually said they were sick of the new direction and left. Years later one of those who left came back and repented. He saw what God was doing and asked the Lord "why didn't you do that with us?' He said he heard the Lord say, "you had the opportunity to be a part of it and you rejected it."

I have seen this scenario played out numerous times. It breaks my heart for many reasons. The most obvious is that I am convinced that it is the story of each one of us at different times. I know the heart of God's people, and it is to be in the center of His will. Yet, many times we do not have the wisdom to embrace the opportunities God sets before us because they often reside outside of the limits that we have created. The good news is that God is very adept at leading us beyond our self-imposed limitations. I praise God that He is both the author and completer of our faith. He is able to Father His Children but cooperation is definitely recommended. As Paul said:

"For if we would judge ourselves, we would not be judged. But when we are judged, we are chastened by the Lord, that we may not be condemned with the world." (1 Co 11:31-32 NKJV)

I know that God will complete His work in us, but as far as I am concerned I would like to learn as many things that I can the easy way rather than the hard way. Unfortunately that hasn't been my track record. It is a prayer of mine that I would receive instruction and obey rather than be instructed by the rod. I know that many of the mistakes that I have made, if people will let me, I can help them to not make the same ones. The reciprocal is true. Many of the mistakes that I am on a collision course for making, if I receive the ministry of others who probably already made them I may have a chance of avoiding them. Hence the relay race.

Growing to maturity is like climbing a mountain. The top of the mountain is the church in maturity. We are all called to climb this mountain with all of our might. We will be able to go the greatest distance when we work as a team, which is the church. It is God's desire that we all be connected to life-giving church. Many people are paddling away and making little progress. God's desire for each one of us is that we would progress rapidly because we are part of a kingdom team. So many are disconnected and often become burned out. There are even many people who are born again and fall away because they never get connected to the type of church where growth is natural. We all have a mandate from God to build the kind of church that is designed for people to come to maturity instead of holding them in immaturity.

There is power in kingdom unity to bring the church to maturity.

Our goal is to climb and build an escalator as we go. The point is that we have the opportunity to cause those who come after us to start at a higher level than we did. They may walk in a greater kingdom manifestation than we do, but we may have actually climbed more of the mountain than they will.

This is seen many times in Scripture. Just as an example, think of Elijah and Elisha. Elijah came to maturity in the time of Ahab and Jezebel. It was a time of great spiritual darkness. Just look how scripture describes it.

"Now Ahab the son of Omri did evil in the sight of the Lord, more than all who were before him. And it came to pass, as though it had been a trivial thing for him to walk in the sins of Jeroboam the son of Nebat, that he took as wife Jezebel the daughter of Ethbaal, king of the Sidonians; and he went and served Baal and worshiped him. Then he set up an altar for Baal in the temple of Baal, which he had built in Samaria. And Ahab made a wooden image. Ahab did more to provoke the Lord God of Israel to anger than all the kings of Israel who were before him." (1 Ki 16:30-33 NKJV)

That little summery barely does it justice. It connects Ahab to a history of growing idolatry among the people of God. If there is a mountain of wickedness in Israel, then Ahab climbs that mountain like a champion. To get an idea of how bad it is, look at two references to his wife Jezebel.

> "For so it was, while Jezebel massacred the prophets of the Lord, that Obadiah had taken one hundred prophets and hidden them, fifty to a cave, and had fed them with bread and water.)" (1 Ki 18:4 NKJV)

The type of witchcraft working through Jezebel always oppresses the prophetic anointing. In order for false religion to flourish the true prophets of God must be silent. When this happens the spirit of revelation becomes rare and people's experience of religion is cut off from a real relationship with the living God. Instead of having fellowship with the God of life and truth they end up having fellowship with the lies of darkness. Here the prophets of God were silent because Jezebel put them to death.

> "Now therefore, send and gather all Israel to me on Mount Carmel, the four hundred and fifty prophets of Baal, and the four hundred prophets of Asherah, who eat at Jezebel's table.'" (1 Ki 18:19 NKJV)

She actually had a great number of pagan prophets who ate at her family's table. The times were really bleak. There was great spiritual darkness and even demonic oppression enough to weary the greatest of saints. Just look at Elijah after he has caused drought for years, had a glorious revival at Mt. Carmel, and caused it to rain. After all of these victories that are too wonderful to begin to examine here, we find Elijah running for his life at the threats of Jezebel.

> "And there he went into a cave, and spent the night in that place; and behold, the word of the Lord came to him, and He said to him, "What are you doing here, Elijah?" So he said, "I have been very zealous for the Lord God of hosts; for the children of Israel have forsaken Your covenant, torn down Your altars, and killed Your prophets with the sword. I alone am left; and they seek to take my life."" (1 Ki 19:9-10 NKJV)

He feels like he is the only one left even though there were 7000 that God says never kissed the mouth of Baal. The people of God are disconnected and going at it alone. Even after one of the most glorious moments of God's glory in human history, Elijah finds himself discouraged and disillusioned. Look at what he had to pay for climbing the mountain of God: he came to maturity in the context of a disconnected church under heavy spiritual darkness. He came to maturity in a church with little light and look at the cost!

Now look at Elisha. He comes to maturity under Elijah's ministry. Look at what he had to pay for a double portion of Elijah's anointing. Elijah goes down in my book as one of the all time great mountain climbers. Not only did he run a good race, but he paved the way for those who came after him to walk in greater glory. Few in the old covenant ever saw the miracles and manifestations of God as Elisha and he was the benefactor of Elijah the great mountain climber!

Scriptures have more to say on the subject.

"Now, therefore, you are no longer strangers and foreigners, but fellow citizens with the saints and members of the household of God, having been built on the foundation of the apostles and prophets, Jesus Christ Himself being the chief cornerstone, in whom the whole building, being fitted together, grows into a holy temple in the Lord, in whom you also are being built together for a dwelling place of God in the Spirit." (Eph 2:19-22 NKJV)

Notice that we are being built together for a dwelling place of God in the Spirit. We are being built into the temple of God. This is the race we are running; this is the mountain we are climbing.

"Do you not know that you are the temple of God and that the Spirit of God dwells in you? If anyone defiles the temple of God, God will destroy him. For the temple of God is holy, which temple you are." (1 Co 3:16-17 NKJV)

So many use this scripture as a proof text for why Christians are not supposed to smoke tobacco or drink alcohol. There is something about this scripture that I want you to see that is very often overlooked. In Greek every "you" in this passage is plural. You could legitimately translate it "Do you all not know that together you are the temple of God and that the Spirit of God dwells in your midst?" There is no way to get around it; there is no place for individualism in the Kingdom of God. Christianity is a team sport. There is no other way for the church to fulfill the mandate given to us by Jesus than for us all to work together and do our part.

Born into the wilderness

One day I was in a ministry team meeting and we were all sharing various things. At that time I was excited about the spiritual journey into maturity. Uncharacteristically of me, I was sharing very little. As soon as I began to share it was like a bomb was dropped in the room. There was one little sentence I said that set some people off. Personally, I was very encouraged by it, but before I got a chance to explain it people were up in arms. What I said was, "when we are born again we are born into the wilderness." The point that I was trying to make is that the experience we have when we are first born again is just the beginning, and although it is often very glorious, it is the glory of a new born babe and not the glory of a mature son of God.

The birth of Israel as a nation teaches us of our personal spiritual journey. They were slaves in Egypt that were brought to birth as a nation when they passed through the Red Sea. That is typological of baptism and of being born again. They were delivered from the type of the kingdom of darkness into the covenant people of God. They were born as a nation but they were still a baby. They still had a slave mentality. They were still filled with idols and immorality. They have yet to grow up. They were called to go into the Promised Land, which is a type of coming to spiritual maturity. The wilderness they wandered through from the Red Sea to the Promised Land is a period where the Hebrews matured. The wilderness is the time and place where people come to maturity.

If we examine all of God's heroes of faith we see that they all had to go through the wilderness; so do we all today. There were a great multitude of men who came out of Egypt, and yet only two men of that original generation were able to make it into the Promised Land. Most of those who were "born again" or baptized through the Red Sea perished in the wilderness. They never made it to the Promised Land or spiritual maturity. Many in the church today who have been born again never make it to spiritual maturity. Many perish in the wilderness.

"For who, having heard, rebelled? Indeed, was it not all who came out of Egypt, led by Moses? Now with whom was He angry forty years? Was it not with those who sinned, whose corpses fell in the wilderness? And to whom did He swear that they would not enter His rest, but to those who did not obey? So we see that they could not enter in because of unbelief. Therefore, since a promise remains of entering His rest, let us fear lest any of you seem to have come short of it. For indeed the gospel was preached to us as well as to them; but the word which they heard did not profit them, not being mixed with faith in those who heard it. For we who have believed do enter that rest, as He has said: "So I swore in My wrath, 'They shall not enter My rest,'" although the works were finished from the foundation of the world." (Heb 3:16-4:3 NKJV)

They were unable to enter into their inheritance because of unbelief. The gospel was preached to us as well as to them, but it didn't profit them because although they heard the gospel they didn't mix it with faith.

Yet there were two who were of a different spirit than the multitude that perished in the wilderness. They were Joshua and Caleb. When God commanded the Israelites to go in and posses the land He promised to give them, the testimony of the multitude was "we would be like grasshoppers in a land of giants," but the testimony of these two was essentially "let us go in according to the Word of God for He is giving it to us." Those who believe enter into His rest.

We are at a place where the church will come to maturity. It is a revival of the life of Christ in the church. There is a formula that I call the revival formula. It seems everyone is looking for a formula, especially for revival, so I decided to postulate one. The formula goes like this:

Repentance precedes revival which precedes harvest.

Repentance in many ways is laying down our controversy with God and simply believing and obeying His Word. Such repentance causes revival, and such revival leads to harvest. So many speak of revival as seeing people born again but the word literally means to live again. How can that which has always been spiritually dead live again? They need vival not revival. No, the church needs revival, we need the life and faith that was originally delivered to the saints by Jesus to be restored. Such life will cause there to be a harvest of souls.

It is stunningly simple yet stunningly profound. Whenever we simply believe God's Word, His life is manifested and bears fruit in us. Whenever people truly repent of new covenant transgression they will experience a revival of the life of Christ that will in turn cause people to be born again. Every area in our life both individually and corporately where we experience revival because we hear, believe and obey God's word will cause life to flow to the world.

Jesus did a perfect job of imparting His life into the world, but doctrines of deceitful spirits began to work to try to snuff out that life. If we look at the first generation apostles we see how wonderfully Jesus reproduced His life in His church. He took those first apostles and set them on the mountain of the Lord. History then experienced a time of mountain sliders until we reached the dark ages. When everything looked bleak, suddenly revelation, repentance and revival started taking off. Let me make it clear that there have been individuals and movements who have been a testimony in the earth and saw spiritual maturity throughout all ages, but we are looking at the overall picture of things. During the dark ages it appeared like the kingdom could have been cut off forever, then a word sounded throughout the earth proclaiming "we are saved by grace through faith apart from works lest any man should boast." That message brought forth new covenant repentance. People turned away from approaching God through works and began approaching God on the grounds of the blood of Jesus and a revival broke out that swept multitudes into the kingdom of God. Wherever people repent and believe there will be revival of the life of Christ.

"Go therefore and make disciples of all the nations, baptizing them in the name of the Father and of the Son and of the Holy Spirit," (Mt 28:19 NKJV)

We are called to make disciples of all nations, baptizing them in the name of God the Father, Son and Holy Spirit. While I am not going to look at the ritual itself, I want to bring something out about this mandate. First there is one God. Second His name expresses all that He is. Third, baptizing means to bring someone into the life of something. Notice in Hebrews that when it refers to the doctrine of baptisms that it is in the plural. Jesus, after He was baptized in the Jordan spoke of an up and coming baptism. He was referring to His death on the cross. The point I want to emphasize is that we have a mandate to make disciples bringing people into life of God as Father, God as Son, and God as Holy Spirit.

We could refer to these as:

Seeing people brought into the life of God the Son, Jesus as their savior.

Seeing people brought into the life of God the Holy Spirit, baptism in the Spirit.

Seeing people brought into the life of God the Father, Christians brought to spiritual maturity.

We could go further to draw parallels between these and the three feasts of Israel and the three parts of the temple. It is well worth examining in depth elsewhere but just to whet the appetite, we can connect Jesus as savior with the feast of Passover and with the outer court of the temple. Notice that the feast of Passover is in the first month of the religious calendar and notice that the light in the outer court is natural sunlight. Similarly, our spiritual life begins when we are born again and that by simply being born again we still see and minister by the light of nature. The next part, the baptism of the Holy Spirit we can connect with the feast of Pentecost and with the inner court of the temple. The feast of Pentecost is the first fruit guarantee that looks toward the full harvest coming in. The light of the inner court is the golden candlestick that burns oil. This speaks of seeing by the anointing of the Spirit. Both of these two realities were available during the Old Covenant for people but the third is actually only available on this side of the cross. This is seeing people come to maturity as sons of God. This connects with the feast of tabernacles and with the Holy of Holies. The feast of tabernacles speaks of the dwelling of God with man and the union of heaven and earth. It begins the civil calendar and therefore speaks of the reign of the kingdom of God. It is connected to the Holy of Holies where the light is the very glory of God. This is the way that Jesus made open. Depending on the light we are operating under, there will be different manifestations. We never leave one level completely behind; we simply build on it.

What we refer to today as the reformation were people seeing the great truth of justification by faith. Hallelujah for that glorious revival! It brought many into the kingdom. Then, we have seen a great and glorious revival known often as sanctification by faith which is connected to the Baptism of the Holy Spirit. This has brought great revival and harvest to the earth. Now God is working and birthing the greatest revival of history which will see the sons of God come forth in maturity on the earth.

Each one of these great revivals has been connected to hearing and believing the Word of God. That is exactly what many have done and they experienced the wonderful life of it. When many of the truths of these moves of God first appeared, there were great birth pains and crises, especially among the true people of God. Never the less, Jesus is the great author of this whole thing, and He will bring it through to completion.

One thing I want to make clear is that there is both a personal and a corporate expression of the wilderness and the Promised Land. Let us go back and look at Moses. He spent 40 years on the back side of the desert before he came forth in maturity. When he did, his ministry delivered Israel from Egypt. His was a personal maturing, and it resulted in a harvest where many were born again. Looking all the way forward to the time of Jesus, we see that He came to maturity and then His ministry birthed the church in Acts. Similarly, in the way Adam was created, we see those first apostles bearing the fruit of maturity from the first day of the new creation. In that first church there were those who were spiritually mature and those who were brand new babes in Christ. As more and more people come to spiritual maturity, we can expect many to be born again. In the midst of all of this we are to look forward to the day when we all come to the measure of the stature of the fullness of Christ! It will come!

Let us look at the life of Moses for more instruction concerning the wilderness. Notice that when Moses was born, God was already at work in his life for a purpose.

"Now there arose a new king over Egypt, who did not know Joseph. And he said to his people, "Look, the people of the children of Israel are more and mightier than we; come, let us deal shrewdly with them, lest they multiply, and it happen, in the event of war, that they also join our enemies and fight

against us, and so go up out of the land.""" (Ex
1:8-10 NKJV)

They certainly dealt shrewdly with them! They
understood that these people would continue to grow
and that it would actually end the way of life that
they were enjoying. The people of God were slaves
and were serving the kingdom of Pharaoh, who was
prospering by their bondage. Yet the natural way with
the Kingdom of God is growth that will eventually
break the wineskin and cause the bubble to burst. The
Egyptians understood that if God's people continued
to grow, their prosperity at the Hebrew's expense
would come to an end and therefore resorted to insid-
ious tactics to keep the people of God in bondage
as slaves. The most important of these tactics was
to develop a slave mentality in the people of God
that is reinforced through wicked works. They were
working to build the house of the enemy of God.

Yet God is with His people, and He has a purpose
that He intends shall come to pass. God's purpose
included delivering Israel from the Land of Egypt.
He had already promised it years ago to Abraham. He
told them beforehand all that would come to pass.

"Then He said to Abram: "Know certainly
that your descendants will be strangers in a
land *that is* not theirs, and will serve them,
and they will afflict them four hundred years.
And also the nation whom they serve I will
judge; afterward they shall come out with
great possessions." (Ge 15:13-14 NKJV)

Even Joseph, who was miraculously raised up by God to govern Egypt actually kept his eyes on this covenant promise of God. Even though he had it very well, and so did God's people in Egypt under his ministry, he looked for the day Israel would leave. Joseph did not try to create a permanent home for Israel in Egypt. He certainly had the means to try, but his eyes were on the Promised Land.

"And Joseph said to his brethren, "I am dying; but God will surely visit you, and bring you out of this land to the land of which He swore to Abraham, to Isaac, and to Jacob." Then Joseph took an oath from the children of Israel, saying, "God will surely visit you, and you shall carry up my bones from here." So Joseph died, being one hundred and ten years old; and they embalmed him, and he was put in a coffin in Egypt." (Ge 50:24-26 NKJV)

For 400 years the Israelites were aliens in a foreign land. They eventually came under heavy slavery and oppression, yet all of those years Joseph was with them waiting for the deliverance God promised. Even in death he testified that God will deliver you from the house of bondage. Even more, He testified not only will God deliver you from the house of bondage, but He will bring you into the Promised Land. All of those years in the wilderness where the majority of those who came out of Egypt died, many could have accused Moses of being a false prophet because he proclaimed that God would bring them into their inheritance and they never saw it in the flesh. During that time in the wilderness, Joseph was still testifying that God would fulfill His word. Not only did Joshua and Caleb enter the Promised Land because they believed the testimony of God, but Joseph also even in death went in with them. God will fulfill every promise He makes.

So we see that God is with His people although they are slaves. Even as slaves the hand of God is evident with Israel. The Egyptians are actually afraid of Israel, their slaves. Israel has no clue what is going on in the minds of those who oppress them. The Egyptians are actually in bondage to fear because they know even more than Israel the power that Israel possesses from a natural perspective. Yet Egypt is blind to the real power that is with the people of God, for if they had eyes to see, they would have been able to read the signs. No matter how shrewd the strategies were, how wicked and calculated for success in the flesh, they were powerless to curse the people whom God has blessed. They should have seen that there is a power at work in these people of which they know not of. It is the power of God. Look at what Egypt tried to do and look how it actually turns out.

> "Therefore they set taskmasters over them to afflict them with their burdens. And they built for Pharaoh supply cities, Pithom and Raamses. But the more they afflicted them, the more they multiplied and grew. And they were in dread of the children of Israel. So the Egyptians made the children of Israel serve

with rigor. And they made their lives bitter with hard bondage— in mortar, in brick, and in all manner of service in the field. All their service in which they made them serve was with rigor." (Ex 1:11-14 NKJV)

It didn't work. Israel continued to multiply. Therefore they resorted to more carnal tactics and commanded that the Hebrew midwives kill any child that is born a male. The problem is that the Hebrew midwives can see that God is with Israel and refused to kill the Lord's anointed. Human wisdom would say that such disobedience to Pharaoh would result in their death, but instead, they come under the blessing of Israel.

"Therefore God dealt well with the midwives, and the people multiplied and grew very mighty. And so it was, because the midwives feared God, that He provided households for them. So Pharaoh commanded all his people, saying, "Every son who is born you shall cast into the river, and every daughter you shall save alive."" (Ex 1:20-22 NKJV)

It was in this context that Moses was born, and instead of drowning him in the river, they kept him alive. When he could no longer be hid they made an ark and put him in the river and he ends up being adopted by Pharaoh's daughter. Who are these people? Moses grows up as a prince of Egypt. Everything the enemy tries to do to destroy the work of God turns out for his destruction. Just ask Haman who tried to annihilate the Jews in the book of Esther, or the devil who thought he won when Jesus was crucified.

So Moses grows up in the palace and in privilege. He could have easily lived and died a carnally satisfied man in that context. Yet listen to his testimony:

> "By faith Moses, when he became of age, refused to be called the son of Pharaoh's daughter, choosing rather to suffer affliction with the people of God than to enjoy the passing pleasures of sin, esteeming the reproach of Christ greater riches than the treasures in Egypt; for he looked to the reward." (Heb 11:24-26 NKJV)

A true hero of faith! He saw in those slaves something that was of more value than all of the treasures of Egypt. He interacted with people of privilege and influence, and to such people Hebrew slaves were probably barely considered people. Yet Moses saw that which is invisible; he saw that God was with these people. He heard the living testimony from the dead bones of Joseph. He saw how all the science of oppression failed because God is with the slaves. He could see by faith that he was being raised up for their deliverance. There is a point where coincidence can no longer be a valid explanation. The river that was to condemn him to death became his entrance into the palace. I am sure he saw that he came to the palace "for such a time as this." He saw that he was called to deliver Israel, but the problem is that he still had a slave mentality. Not the slave mentality of his brothers in the flesh, but the mentality of those who were slaves in sin yet prosperous in the world of the Egyptians. Instead of doing things in the power of God, his first attempts to fulfill his calling were done in the power of the flesh and it was disastrous. Instead of it succeeding, it actually turned out to be a failure. Why? Because Moses needs to go into the wilderness to get Egypt out of Israel (out of Moses) so that he can return in the power of God and get Israel out of Egypt!

Certainly Moses was right about his calling. He sincerely wanted to be used by God to deliver the Hebrews from Egypt. The problem is that things didn't work out how he imagined they would. While his heart was in the right place his methods and power that he relied upon were not. This has been one of the greatest birth pains in the church: to get our methods and power right. Our hearts have been in the right place, but instead of operating in the power of God we have operated in the power and systems of man. That story ends in failure. Yet the other side of that story is God is at work. Moses had a calling, and he shall fulfill it. Even his failure set in motion his journey into the wilderness that will eventually lead to the fulfillment of God's promises. God is at work in His people to bring to pass all that He has promised. Even our failures are God's opportunities.

It was there, from the back side of the desert that Moses returned in the power of God. It was from the wilderness that David returned to reign as king. It was from the wilderness that Jesus returned and demonstrated the kingdom of God. It was from the wilderness that Paul returned and operated in the power of God. All of God's servants who want to carry the power of God must go through the wilderness, and so will the church!

"Who is this coming up from the wilderness, Leaning upon her beloved?" (So 8:5a NKJV)

The bride in the Song of Songs goes through a journey from immaturity to maturity. It is the story of us becoming mature in love. Here is a prophetic picture for each one of us and for the church. The Bride is coming out of the wilderness! She is coming into the Promised Land! How is she coming? She is leaning on her beloved. She is broken of her own power and wisdom and is now leaning on the Lord. She trusts the Word of God who is Jesus. She is coming in the power of God. The sons of God are coming to maturity.

Apostolic weakness

—〰—

One of the key elements of our coming to maturity and operating in the power of God is weakness.

> "And He said to me, "My grace is sufficient for you, for My strength is made perfect in weakness." Therefore most gladly I will rather boast in my infirmities, that the power of Christ may rest upon me. Therefore I take pleasure in infirmities, in reproaches, in needs, in persecutions, in distresses, for Christ's sake. For when I am weak, then I am strong." (2 Co 12:9-10 NKJV)

Notice that Paul says that he would rather boast in his infirmities so that the power of Christ may rest upon him. It appears that he has an obsession to walk in the power of God. It is the thing that Paul so esteems that he actually takes pleasure in everything that helps keep him in the power of God. If you actually ponder it, it seems crazy. Paul is taking pleasure in things that are completely un-pleasurable. He sees that these are the contexts that cause people to walk in the power of God.

I have had numerous experiences of weakness that resulted in power, but certainly not as many as Paul. I mentioned previously how, when I was a missionary pastor, I found myself one time (actually numerous times) without means to provide for my family. I went to the prayer room because I had no natural recourse, and there the Lord caused me to repent, and then He met my needs.

Another time God met my need when I went to Zambia and Burkina Faso. Robert Mearns, who oversees our work, told me to be praying about what we should be doing next. During the process the Lord showed me that I was to go to Africa. I went and told Stephanie and she said "I know, He already told me." I mentioned that I didn't have any invitations, but if that was what the Lord wanted He would make it happen. Within a week two invitations came to minister in Africa. When I first researched what it would cost to go, I decided I wouldn't go. For two weeks the Spirit of the Lord dealt severely with me. Previous to this experience the Lord had told me to go somewhere and I hadn't because I felt I didn't have the financial resources to do so. Over a year later I found out what was going on where the Lord told me to go, and I knew that I had missed a very important kingdom engagement. I promised the Lord that if He ever told me to go somewhere again I would go no matter what, and here I was doing the same thing again. Finally I gathered a couple friends and repented before the Lord and went. After I made the decision, the Lord told me that the provision for the trip wouldn't come from Africa and it wouldn't come until I returned. I went, and upon my return, several people who didn't know what I was doing actually sent rather large sums of money!

Another time when I went to Nigeria, I went and I probably had a total of $400 to my name and less than that with me on the trip. As a matter of fact, I barely had more than $200 that someone gave me just before I left. I was working in Ibadan Nigeria with a friend who has a wonderful ministry there. They provide medical care to people who can't afford it. Because of this work they are having evangelistic success among the natives of Nigeria who are relatively unconverted. He and his family have made very real sacrifices for this work, and they were living in a home that had no water or electricity. In their place it had rats and roaches. His place cost about $200 per year; for $500 per year more he would be able to get a nice place that was very clean and had water and electricity. I told him that I would give him $500 for the house but that he would have to wait until I returned home so I could save it up for him.

While I was working with him, I was invited to minister in a church in Abuja. It would require two internal plane tickets to get us there, and we didn't have the finances to go. I told my friend that if God wanted us there He would get us there. After that I was invited to minister in a church that I was not originally scheduled to minister in. They gave me a gift of money that would give us enough to go to Abuja.

My friend was also given a small amount of money from somewhere else before we left for Abuja.

From my perspective, we were robbed three times on our way to the airport in Lagos. What happened in my opinion is nothing less than robbery. First we were at a stop light and a man ran up to the car and suddenly it began smoking. He got my friend out of the car and convinced him that it needed a repair. As he spoke, he pulled out a wrench and ran off with a part of the engine. He came back and he demanded a considerably large sum for the part and labor which I think was set up all along. Next we were pulled over by a police officer and we had to give him money to let us go. That is something they do to subsidize their income. They pull people over for no reason and require money in order to be released. When we got to the airport, we put all of our money together and we didn't have enough to get the plane ticket any more. I had one 20 pound note left that I was saving for the journey home. I exchanged it for a terrible rate and had about $3 more than we needed for the plane tickets. When we were paying for the plane tickets, we counted out the money with the agent for one ticket. When we were counting the money for the other ticket, his friend, whom he had handed the money to, said that we were short on the amount for the first ticket. We knew that we had given him the correct money, and he had pocketed it yet there was nothing we could do. I told my friend that the Lord wants us on that plane and that somewhere on us was the money we needed to finish buying the tickets. We searched our luggage, and my friend found a crumpled up bill in a jacket pocket. We paid for our tickets and left to get on the plane without enough money to even buy water! We didn't know what we were going to find when we got to Abuja but we were to be there for three days. I told my friend that God must have something very special for us in Abuja. When we got there they had a dinner prepared, and it was incredible. Then they put us up in a very nice hotel where the president stays, and we each had our own room that included two king sized beds in each one. We were told to eat at the hotel and put it on the room tab. We had a wonderful time, and we were broke! When we went to return, he gave me enough money to give my friend the $500 I promised and enough to get us home as well. Praise Jesus!

If I had been in a place financially where I had no need for the power of God, I would not have seen the power of God in action. Having lack, however, is not the same as poverty of spirit. There are many ways that we need the power of God. Awareness of our needs is the first step in seeing God's power meet our needs. Awareness of lack is therefore important, but it is looking to God in humility and faith that plugs into the power of God.

I have heard many people longingly speak about how people in other countries see God work in power because they are not as materially well off as people in countries like America and they need God to act or they will starve to death. While this may be true to some degree, we need to see that it is really about people feeling the weight of need and looking to God to meet it. Weakness and brokenness is where God's power is made perfect. What I mean is that when people are struggling to put food on the table, they look to the Lord they find the power of God to put food on their table. Yet, God wants to break that level of living for people. The Word makes it clear that God wants to bless people. God's blessing cannot be an excuse to not walk in the power of God. We need to take personally the great commission so that we feel the burden of it in a way where we need God to act. I do not know if Martin Luther, John Knox, John Wesley, Charles Finney or many other heroes of religion had great financial need, but what they had was a desperate burden for the kingdom of God and a humble faith in God that caused His power to be manifested. There are so many things that if we will take responsibility for them and break before the Lord we will see His power rise to the occasion. We could easily be burdened for the spiritual apathy, moral degradation, social injustice or a multitude of other very important kingdom issues. We could cry like John Knox "Give me (my nation) or I die!" Such a position with faith will see the power of God in action. If you really want to see it up close, carry people's burdens to the Lord in faith and prayer. Weep over people who are hurting, who are lost, who are in bondage. Wrestle for the needs of people, and you will see God step up to the challenge! Don't just give lip service and say a few trite prayers, let the weight of it consume you until the burden is so great you can't bear it and see the wonderful power of God work it out before your eyes.

Often, when I hear people speak about how God is able to work miracles in other countries because of their desperate situations, they make reference to Africa. I have worked with many Africans, and have been to Africa several times. The reason God is able to work miracles in Africa is not simply because they have poverty. There is poverty everywhere, even in the USA just as there is affluence among Africans. It is not simply because they are in desperate situations that God acts. There are many people in desperate situations all over the world. What I discovered is that Africans have humility before authority. I often see them respecting and serving with diligence their elders and superiors in the flesh. When they think of God, they see the God who by the Word of His power created the heavens and earth. They see Jesus on the throne and believe He has the power and authority to act. They believe in His power and authority more than any earthy power or authority. Such a perspective enriches our understanding of brokenness. Pride is self sufficient and believes in its own power and ability, brokenness and humility looks elsewhere hopefully to the God who saves: Jesus.

> "Now when Jesus had entered Capernaum, a centurion came to Him, pleading with Him, saying, "Lord, my servant is lying at home paralyzed, dreadfully tormented." And Jesus said to him, "I will come and heal him." The centurion answered and said, "Lord, I am not worthy that You should come under my roof. But only speak a word, and my servant

will be healed. For I also am a man under authority, having soldiers under me. And I say to this *one,* 'Go,' and he goes; and to another, 'Come,' and he comes; and to my servant, 'Do this,' and he does *it.*" When Jesus heard *it,* He marveled, and said to those who followed, "Assuredly, I say to you, I have not found such great faith, not even in Israel!" (Mt 8:5-10 NKJV)

This centurion actually causes Jesus to marvel at his faith. Such faith touches the heart of God. He was in a desperate situation which he was powerless change. In brokenness and faith He turned to Jesus who has the power to deal with the situation. He sees Jesus as one having authority to heal his servant. He himself was a man of authority, and he connects his authority to the fact that he is under authority. In this sense he is exercising delegated authority. He sees Jesus as under the authority of God, and hence has the authority to act as His representative. (Even though Jesus is God, he ministered as a man anointed with the Holy Spirit and in obedience to His Father.) Since Jesus has actual authority in the centurions mind, all he has to do is speak and it shall come to pass. Such a humility and brokenness is a recipe for the power of God. It is a perception of Jesus as lord and king upon His throne exercising authority by the Word of His power. A decree from the throne of God brings to pass whatever is decreed.

It is only when our brokenness and humility looks to the God revealed in scriptures that we plug into the power of God. If we look to to any other god other than the God revealed in scripture there is no power.

> ""What profit is the image, that its maker should carve it, The molded image, a teacher of lies, That the maker of its mold should trust in it, To make mute idols? Woe to him who says to wood, 'Awake!' To silent stone, 'Arise! It shall teach!' Behold, it is overlaid with gold and silver, Yet in it there is no breath at all. "But the Lord is in His holy temple. Let all the earth keep silence before Him."" (Hab 2:18-20 NKJV)

People often put their hope in gods other than the God of scriptures. Sometimes it is naïve faith in the inherent goodness of humanity. Others trust in the power of humanity. Some new agers believe in the power of faith in and of itself and not in Jesus. There are all kinds of gods that people put their trust in, including government, education, money, and multitudes of false religions but there in only one God who has power to save and His name is Jesus. The good news is that He actually has power to save, and it is manifested when people walk in humility, brokenness and faith. It is God's desire that His power to save would be manifested in His people.

This passion of Paul for the power of God marked his ministry.

> "And I, brethren, when I came to you, did not come with excellence of speech or of wisdom

declaring to you the testimony of God. For I determined not to know anything among you except Jesus Christ and Him crucified. I was with you in weakness, in fear, and in much trembling. And my speech and my preaching were not with persuasive words of human wisdom, but in demonstration of the Spirit and of power, that your faith should not be in the wisdom of men but in the power of God." (1 Co 2:1-5 NKJV)

Paul has a burden that people will have an encounter with the power of God. He wants men's faith not to rest in the wisdom of men but in the power of God. He certainly could have used all kinds of human means that are calculated to get a certain result and they can certainly get a result but it will still be built by the flesh. It will not last. Robert Mearns likes to say that "God doesn't appreciate what he doesn't initiate." Crudely put, God will not tolerate that which is illegitimate. If it isn't born of Him, if it isn't born of His seed, He will not acknowledge ownership of it.

"Having been born again, not of corruptible seed but incorruptible, through the word of God which lives and abides forever, because "All flesh is as grass, And all the glory of man as the flower of the grass. The grass withers, And its flower falls away, But the word of the Lord endures forever." Now this is the word

which by the gospel was preached to you." (1
Pe 1:23-25 NKJV)

Everything that is not built by the Spirit is illegitimate. It may actually sprout up and appear more
glorious than something that is legitimate at first, but
eventually it will die. So many people do not know
how to build with the power of God, but they do
know how to build with the flesh. They do not realize
that such works, no matter how sincere they are or
how effective they seem, are actually out of bounds.
Just think about Moses when he first tries to deliver
Israel; he was operating in the power of flesh rather
than the power of God. He was very blessed that his
work of the flesh never succeeded. So many times
when men build a work through the flesh it succeeds.
Anything that is built carnally requires flesh to maintain it. Eventually it will go the way of all flesh and
die. The temple will not be made through human
hands but through the hand of God.

""And you shall speak to the children of
Israel, saying: 'This shall be a holy anointing
oil to Me throughout your generations. It
shall not be poured on man's flesh; nor shall
you make any other like it, according to its
composition. It is holy, and it shall be holy
to you. Whoever compounds any like it, or
whoever puts any of it on an outsider, shall
be cut off from his people.'"" (Ex 30:31-33
NKJV)

Notice how the anointing oil will not be poured out on any flesh. People can try to compound something like it and it might appear to be the true anointing, but it isn't; it is a counterfeit. Such things are cut off from the kingdom of God. This is why Paul would not rely upon words of human wisdom. God will not anoint that which trusts in the power of man. It will build an illegitimate work. People's faith will not be based on an encounter with the power of God but upon the work of the flesh. Such works are eventually doomed to fail.

"For we are God's fellow workers; you are God's field, you are God's building. According to the grace of God which was given to me, as a wise master builder I have laid the foundation, and another builds on it. But let each one take heed how he builds on it. For no other foundation can anyone lay than that which is laid, which is Jesus Christ. Now if anyone builds on this foundation with gold, silver, precious stones, wood, hay, straw, each one's work will become clear; for the Day will declare it, because it will be revealed by fire; and the fire will test each one's work, of what sort it is. If anyone's work which he has built on it endures, he will receive a reward. If anyone's work is burned, he will suffer loss; but he himself will be saved, yet so as through fire." (1 Co 3:9-15 NKJV)

Every man's works will be tested with fire; if they are able to endure the fire they will receive a reward. If not, they will still be saved if they are on the foundation of Christ, but as through fire. I would much rather examine my works to see what nature they are of and, if necessary, tear them down and start all over. I do not want to live my life and build something that is pleasing to the flesh but not acknowledged by God. Just taking these passages seriously as the Word of God should be plenty to get weakness working in our life.

Notice that the source of the power of God is Christ crucified. This is absolutely true in every way. From every angle the center of the power of God is Christ crucified. Our sins are forgiven right there. We are born again right there. We were united with him right there, and we went into death that leads to resurrection life right there. The handwriting of the law was cancelled there. The curse of sin was broken there. Our old man was crucified there. The body of sin was killed right there. The devil was defeated right there! Every blessing, healing, deliverance, and form of salvation is simply a manifestation in the flesh of what has already taken place at Calvary! There is so much power for the church to operate in when we quit putting our trust in the flesh!

We need to see that the gospel is no gospel if there is no power of God being manifested.

"For I will not dare to speak of any of those things which Christ has not accomplished through me, in word and deed, to make the

Gentiles obedient— in mighty signs and
wonders, by the power of the Spirit of God,
so that from Jerusalem and round about to
Illyricum I have fully preached the gospel of
Christ." (Ro 15:18-19 NKJV)

Paul connects mighty signs and wonders by the
power of the Spirit of God to the gospel being fully
preached. If they are not present then the gospel is
only partially preached. At one level this causes great
rejoicing because this is the Christianity that is our
inheritance, but it also causes great brokenness and
weakness because it is only accomplished by the
power of God which is made perfect in weakness. I
want to point out a few things about gospel signs for
a moment.

"And they went out and preached everywhere,
the Lord working with them and confirming
the word through the accompanying signs.
Amen." (Mk 16:20 NKJV)

Signs accompany the preaching of the gospel.
Signs always point to something. Think about it. What
would a confirmation be of a gospel message such as
this: "if you believe Jesus died for your sins and you
receive Him as your savior you will be forgiven and
go to heaven when you die?" It would be going to
heaven when you die. What if the message includes,
"by the blood of Jesus you have complete access
into the presence of God." It would be people experiencing the presence of God and all that goes along

with it. What if the message said, "by his stripes you were healed?" How about "the old man was crucified with Christ and the body of sin done away with?" As Galatians proclaimed, miracles and the supply of the spirit do not come from works of the law but through the hearing of faith. If people do not hear and believe they will never experience the kingdom life. The most important foundation that is not negotiable is that our sins are forgiven at the cross. We must have our names written in the Lamb's book of life. We may live out our lives disconnected from the fullness that is already ours in Christ, that which was given at Calvary, but at least we will be on the foundation of Christ and be saved. The good news is that God actually desires and has freely given us much more in Christ.

Do you see how the revelation of all that Jesus has done at the Cross and faith in it from the heart will cause all kinds of signs and wonders? The types of signs and wonders that accompany the preaching of Christ crucified are too numerous to catalogue. They touch every realm of man and nature. They operate in realms such as the fruit of the spirit and the gifts of the spirit. It is all about life in the Spirit because of Calvary. It takes the power of God to truly forgive, to have joy in trials, to love with God's kind of love. It is the same power that heals the sick, casts out devils, experiences dreams, visions, prophecies, words of knowledge and a whole realm of kingdom manifestations. It is the same cross that heals families, cities and nations. It is the same cross that even affects nature. It is the cross through which all creation is reconciled to God. His kingdom will be manifested in time and nature through faith. It is only when we see what is in the Word and believe from the heart that we shall see the Word manifested in the flesh.

Signs are worked in the name of Jesus. I want to say that they actually declare His character and nature. God heals the sick and does glorious miracles not to prove He is God so that you will worship Him but simply because He loves people. The miracles declare His name. He heals people who are believers and unbelievers because He loves people and He has compassion on them. God forgives because it is in His nature. He gives us joy and peace because it is in His nature. They are demonstrations of His name. They reveal who He is.

"'For the kingdom of God is not in word but in power." (1 Co 4:20 NKJV)

The first generation believers understood this. It is what they held dear and protected. This is the faith that was once and for all delivered unto the saints that we are to contend for. Religion is not meant to be a form without power. We must make the power of God in the church non-negotiable. Look at what happened when the first apostles perceived that the power they were operating in was beginning to decline and look at how they pinpointed the problem and found a solution.

"Therefore, brethren, seek out from among you seven men of good reputation, full of the Holy Spirit and wisdom, whom we may appoint over this business; but we will give ourselves continually to prayer and to the ministry of the word. Then the word of God spread, and the number of the disciples multiplied greatly in Jerusalem, and a great many of the priests were obedient to the faith." (Ac 6:3-4,7 NKJV)

They saw that the power was waning because they became too busy. They didn't have the time to work on the power generator which was prayer and the ministry of the Word. When they went back to the fundamental the power of God came back in full force. All they were doing was keeping the same priorities that we see in Jesus' ministry if we look closely. I do not care what anyone tries to tell me, these are the two great powerhouses of the Kingdom: prayer and the ministry of the Word. Both are foolishness to the ways and means of men, but they are the spiritual capital of the Kingdom of God. True prayer isn't a spiritual devotion to make us feel spiritual and the ministry of the word isn't a quaint 15 minute talk. If we aren't generating spiritual power, we are not what scripture refers to when it speaks of being full of the Spirit. A tree is known by its fruit. If we lack, ask.

Weakness and brokenness are absolutely necessary to the gospel being fully preached. It must be a revelation of the life of Jesus, and that life is only revealed when the veil of the flesh is torn down. It is in death that we find life.

"But Jesus answered them, saying, "The hour has come that the Son of Man should be glorified. Most assuredly, I say to you, unless a grain of wheat falls into the ground and dies, it remains alone; but if it dies, it produces much grain. He who loves his life will lose it, and he who hates his life in this world will keep it for eternal life. If anyone serves Me, let him follow Me; and where I am, there My servant will be also. If anyone serves Me, him My Father will honor." (Jn 12:23-26 NKJV)

This passage is true in so many ways. Some things we see is that the way to see the glory of God is to die to the flesh, to die to carnal reasoning, to die to self centeredness, to die to the world, to die to sin, and to die to the kingdom of darkness. It is all through the cross of Jesus. As long as we love the treasures of Egypt, as long as we seek the approval of men rather than God, as long as we trust in the flesh, as long as we are satisfied with less than what God has called us to, then the glory of God will never be revealed. It is only when we die to ourselves that we will find the life of Christ being revealed in us. To the measure that we have died with Christ is the measure to which He will reveal His life in us. We must die to our pride, we must die to our self reliance, and we must die to selfishness and live in the power and presence of God.

After examining the Biblical standard for Christianity it can make us feel like we will never be able to live up to it. We could water the Scriptures down to fit our experience, but this is not tenable. The standard is immutable. There is only one way that we will ever be able to live up to the Biblical requirements. The answer is the same as it is for everything pertaining to the kingdom of God: faith.

We have faith because He is faithful. We cannot live above the measure of what we have received. If you lack for anything, ask for it in prayer. He will answer real prayer. It is His passion to reveal Himself to us, through us and in us. He is able to do what He has promised He will do. He will conform us into the image of Christ. At the end of the day I must testify that my Daddy is able to rule His house well. He is able to raise up sons to maturity. He has guaranteed it through His Spirit.

> "For all the promises of God in Him *are* Yes, and in Him Amen, to the glory of God through us. Now He who establishes us with you in Christ and has anointed us *is* God, who also has sealed us and given us the Spirit in our hearts as a guarantee." (2 Co 1:20-22 NKJV)

> "In Him you also *trusted,* after you heard the word of truth, the gospel of your salvation; in whom also, having believed, you were sealed with the Holy Spirit of promise, who is the guarantee of our inheritance until the redemption of the purchased possession, to the praise of His glory." (Eph 1:13-14 NKJV)

The saints at Corinth go down as some of my all time favorites. They were babies in Christ with dirty diapers but they had the seal of the Spirit. They had the guarantee that God would complete the work in them that He began. That is what the baptism of the Holy Spirit is, it is a guarantee that the full harvest will come in. It is the guarantee that the life that is in you when you were born again will come forth in maturity. You will be conformed into the image of Christ. Many Christians act like the baptism of the Holy Spirit is the be all end all of Christianity when it is just the seal that God will complete what He began! It is like the cloud by day and the pillar at night that was with the people of God in the wilderness. You could say that was the guarantee that Israel will make it into the Promised Land; that they would come into their inheritance. How can it be prevented if God is in their midst in such a way? So also, we will come to maturity because of His Spirit that dwells in our midst. The baptism of the Holy Spirit is not a sign that we are super-Christians; it is a sign that God will conform us into the image of Christ. There is a spiritual DNA that we receive when we are born again that will come to maturity, but it will happen in the wilderness.

Think for a minute about olives and grapes. There is anointing oil in the olive, and there is refreshing wine in the grape. That is what we want to get at. We only get at it when they are crushed; when they are broken.

"And being in Bethany at the house of Simon the leper, as He sat at the table, a woman came having an alabaster flask of very costly oil of spikenard. Then she broke the flask and poured it on His head." (Mk 14:3 NKJV)

There is anointing oil in the flask, but it is useless until the flask is broken. As long as the flask remains unbroken, the anointing oil cannot get out. There is incredible kingdom power and life in us, but it isn't manifested until the flask is broken. Olives and grapes need to be crushed for their purpose to be revealed. Who does the crushing? It is silly for the olive to say, "I can't wait to be anointing oil, I think I will crush myself." God does the work, and He does it in the wilderness!

I had a tape by Bob Mumford called "Pulling the King's Carriage." He had a vision of wild horses in a field and one day the master came to break the horses. One horse submitted to the master's discipline and was broken. The other horse was very powerful and proud, and after many attempts to break the horse he finally let the horse loose in his fields. That horse boasted about how powerful he was and how he wouldn't let himself be broken. One day that horse looked and there was that other horse. The submissive horse was part of a team who was decked out royally and was pulling the king's carriage. The wild horse looked at the majesty and dignity of those horses and wished he could be a part of that team, but it was already too late. He still belonged to the king, was still loved by him, but he was not fit for the master's use. The same thing is true with us as Christians; we have the opportunity to submit to the discipline of the Lord so that we may be able to pull the king's carriage.

Moses had a calling from his youth and he probably also had his idea of how to accomplish it that was different from God's plan. Moses may have thought God would use all of the training he got in Egypt, but God thought it would be better to use a dead man. God led him out into the wilderness where he became fit for the master's use.

Joseph had a calling, and that calling provoked his brothers to jealousy and eventually led them to sell Joseph into slavery. Later, on the other side of the wilderness, Joseph testified that what his brothers meant for evil God meant for good. Sound like the cross? I am sure that when Joseph received the dreams from God he believed in God's calling on his life, but he probably also had imaginations of how it would work out. He discovered that God's seminary was Potipher's house where he did so well he got promoted to the prison. I can hear him asking, "God, are You sure You aren't reading the blue prints upside down?" Nope, everything is going according to plan.

I am not sure I would like to be mentioned in all the secret counsels of God. Job got the brunt end of a conversation between God and the devil. Actually God had good things planned, but did it really require a cross? I can almost imagine the throne room of heaven when they brought up Jonah.

"hmmm, who should we send to Nineveh? Perhaps Jonah."

"God, even you can't get Jonah there, he hates them. He would rather see them destroyed"

I think God has a sense of humor. He bets on the most unlikely candidates. God doesn't gamble, however, because He stacks the decks. You want to place a bet about Jonah? He is really no challenge after all. I am so encouraged about the story of Jonah. God makes a decision and gives Jonah a mission. Jonah runs the other way and even in running events were set in motion to make him fit for the masters use. He spent three days in the belly of a fish, and after repentance, he came forth in resurrection power. If he hadn't repented he would have perished in the fish. Nineveh actually repented at the preaching of Jonah! May there be many such preachers who have been delivered from the belly of death into resurrection life! God the Father is the one who is ultimately responsible for offering His only begotten son on the cross. Therefore know that it is all God's work. He leads His children to the cross and into resurrection life. The other side of the story is that Jesus submitted willingly and so must we. The end result is resurrection life. Praise Jesus!

When the Bible tells us to count it all joy when we fall into all kinds of diverse trails I think it actually means we are to rejoice. Talk about something so contrary to the wisdom of the world, but by faith we see through the cross to the resurrection. I heard that Martin Luther actually thanked the papist for all of the persecution. He said that while the Word of God told him to trust in the Lord, they actually forced him to do so. God will keep sending the cross to us until we get on it and die. When we do, we will find resurrection life on the other side. Eventually another cross will come until we are completely conformed to His image. To the level that we are humbled with Him in death is to the same measure we will be exalted. So rejoice for great is your reward in heaven.

The Rock of Church

—⟋⟍⟋—

"When Jesus came into the region of Caesarea Philippi, He asked His disciples, saying, "Who do men say that I, the Son of Man, am?" So they said, "Some say John the Baptist, some Elijah, and others Jeremiah or one of the prophets." He said to them, "But who do you say that I am?" Simon Peter answered and said, "You are the Christ, the Son of the living God." Jesus answered and said to him, "Blessed are you, Simon Bar-Jonah, for flesh and blood has not revealed this to you, but My Father who is in heaven. And I also say to you that you are Peter, and on this rock I will build My church, and the gates of Hades shall not prevail against it. And I will give you the keys of the kingdom of heaven, and whatever you bind on earth will be bound in heaven, and whatever you loose on earth will be loosed in heaven."" (Mt 16:13-19 NKJV)

Here Jesus mentions that He will build a church. It is in the heart of God to build church. He is very excited about it. In this story Jesus teaches us much about church.

He begins by asking the disciples "who do men say that I am?"

They give him the latest headlines. Then He asks "who do you say that I am?"

At this point Peter blurts out "You are the Christ the son of the living God!"

Jesus basically says this; "That's it Peter! You got it. By revelation from the Spirit you got it. Remember this. This is the rock upon which I will build my church. My church will be built by the revelation of who I am that is given not through the wisdom of men but through the revelation of the Spirit. Excellent Peter, remember how it came, because I have many more things to show you but you can't handle them right now, but the Holy Spirit will lead you into all truth. Remember how to see me through the revelation of the Spirit because I will build my church through the revelation of who I am given by the Spirit."

No wonder Jesus was excited. This is how the church is built: through the revelation of Jesus by the Spirit. This is the spirit of prophesy, the testimony of Jesus. What do you see through the revelation of the Spirit? Jesus as savior, Jesus as Lord, Jesus as healer, Jesus as deliverer, Jesus who is merciful and gracious slow to anger and rich and love? Who do you see? Seeing is the key to being. As we see him we become like him. That is the way to holiness. That is the way to victory. This is the way by which the gates of hell shall not prevail.

Faith sees possibility where doubt and unbelief see impossibility. So much of the battle is over what we see. We act according to our faith. We can't help it. Before I went to Northern Ireland, I had been part of a successful ministry in the USA. I naively believed that what worked in the USA would have the same impact elsewhere and to some extent it does, but we must realize that the spiritual strong-holds are different wherever we go. Certainly there is much that is universally important wherever we go because much of the kingdom life is built exactly the same. For example, forgiveness is a nonnegotiable. Kingdom essentials must be reproduced everywhere by people who have the substance of kingdom of God. Forgiving people reproduce forgiving people. Generous people reproduce generous people. All life reproduces according to its kind. If you have spiritual life of some type it will reproduce itself in others. The goal is to always be adding more knowledge of Jesus to what we already have. Even if we spend all of our life in one place, if we haven't been completely conformed to the image of Christ then there is still more life to be had. The challenge that we often face is that in order to bring spiritual breakthrough we often need to receive an enlarged revelation of Jesus ourselves. When I found myself in a different context facing different challenges, the knowledge I had of Jesus was insufficient to bear the fruit that I longed to see. I needed to receive more revelation of Jesus personally in order to be fruitful.

Whenever we seek to extend the kingdom of God, we need to overcome the strongholds that are set against it. There are many tactics of the enemy to restrict life and different strongholds are more critical in different places. In one place the battle may be hopelessness, another place discouragement, or busyness, or unforgiveness, maybe self-righteousness, or it may be license to sin. The list could go on. If we want to see real breakthrough we need to overcome the primary strongholds in a region. What I discovered is that if the revelation of Jesus that you have is not sufficient to break through the spiritual climate, then you need to lift your vision higher. Go boldly to the throne of Grace and believe that there is a revelation of Jesus which will break through whatever the kingdom of darkness has set up to rob people of life. Jesus has already overcome all things. He already has the grace to overcome for every possible situation. He has overcome all sin. He has overcome every evil spirit. He has overcome the flesh. He has overcome the world. He wants to work out His victory in our lives!

> "For whatever is born of God overcomes the world. And this is the victory that has overcome the world— our faith. Who is he who overcomes the world, but he who believes that Jesus is the Son of God?" (1 Jn 5:4-5 NKJV)

The wonderful thing is that every time we break-through we are enriched in our vision of who He is and what He has done for us.

I have been in numerous places where I have heard the same story. The people of God will talk about what God is doing around the world and then make excuses why it is too hard for God to do such things where they live. Without realizing it they are releasing their faith in the lies of the devil. In that sense they are having fellowshipping with dark-ness. They are turned away from the Lord and turned toward a lie. They need to turn around. They need to repent! How is it possible that there is any terri-tory, stronghold, sin, or spiritual darkness that is so powerful that Jesus can't break through? I cannot fathom it.

Not only can the kingdom of God breakthrough anywhere, I believe that the way it breaks through is absolutely simple and beautiful. I have become convinced that principalities and powers of darkness are overcome right where they intersect with real life. A person can be home raising the kids, doing the dishes, and overcoming principalities just by having peace and joy in a place where everyone else is living in discouragement and hopelessness. A person can be overturning ancient demonic thrones simply by walking in forgiveness where everyone else is bound by bitterness and un-forgiveness. It is absolutely beautiful!

We have moved many times, and I usually find that you will discover the spiritual warfare simply by observing what starts working against you. We moved into the Shankill Estate in Belfast, and suddenly I saw fear growing in Stephanie that was never there before. Sure, houses were burned down right behind our house, people smashed our windows, and they tore down the fence in our back yard. In the natural there were certainly circumstances that reinforced fear, but if we would have submitted to fear or to frustration for being in such a place we would have broken spiritual fellowship with Jesus. By the grace of God it was there at that house in the Shankill that we met the Lord in ways we never knew Him before. We found Him not in fear but in peace.

There is no way that I can adequately explain how, through simple actions during the course of a normal day that the kingdom of God breaks through. I have been in places where criticism and gossip ran like a disease. By simply walking in forgiveness and love the ruling spirits of the region will actually be evicted. In a place where people are cut off from the presence of God because they judge whether they are pleasing to God by their works, a few people walking in the presence of the Lord because of His work on the cross will actually begin to overturn the demonic thrones of the region! The gates of hell will not prevail against such people.

The keys of the kingdom of heaven are connected to the spiritual revelation of Jesus. In the Greek it actually reads, "Whatever you bind on earth will have *already* been bound in heaven and whatever you loose on earth will have *already* been loosed in heaven." You see the importance of the fact that it is already initiated in heaven? It is simply this, that it is already accomplished. It is already reality, but it becomes manifested in the flesh as people receive the revelation of Jesus. Who can fathom the incredible riches that are already ours in Christ and are about to be revealed as we see and believe?

God will build His church and the gates of hell will be utterly destroyed on the earth. The gates of hell speak of the ruling power of the kingdom of darkness. The cities of darkness are going to be liberated. What is the church? You could call it the gates of heaven, the city of God, where the government of God is manifested, where heaven and earth are wed. The church is the temple of God, where God's presence is manifested, where His glory is revealed. The church is God's house; it is His family where He fathers His children. The list could go on. What is a church? Right now they are an outpost of heaven on earth, and our desire is to see them grow so the kingdom of God will expand and cover the earth. We want to see the kingdom territory grow like Israel grew under David and Solomon. We want to see the nations brought into the obedience of Christ!

One of the things I love is the incredible power of prayer. Think about some of the things scripture testifies concerning prayer. Whatsoever you shall ask believing you shall receive. Ask and you will receive so that your joy may be full. If we ask anything according to His will He hears us and if He hears us we know that we have of Him what we ask. If anyone lacks, let him ask and God will give it to him. We could go on like this but enough is said. Now if these are some of the promises associated with prayer then think about the fact that Jesus taught his disciples to pray for the kingdom of God come and for God's will to be done on earth as it is in heaven. I think that maybe Jesus wants us to pray for this because God intends to answer it. I don't think the Jesus is dangling a carrot from a stick and holding it out so that we will chase it but never reach it. That is just silly. Call me a literalist, but I actually think that Jesus means for the kingdom of God to come and for God's will to be done on earth as it already is in heaven.

I would go so far as to say that everything on earth is at some level either a manifestation of heaven or hell. Often times they are mixed up all in the same field. There are two seeds that are growing in the earth and both will come to maturity.

"Who is wise and understanding among you? Let him show by good conduct that his works are done in the meekness of wisdom. But if you have bitter envy and self-seeking in your hearts, do not boast and lie against the truth. This wisdom does not descend from above, but is earthly, sensual, demonic. For where envy and self-seeking exist, confusion and every evil thing are there. But the wisdom that is from above is first pure, then peaceable, gentle, willing to yield, full of mercy and good fruits, without partiality and without hypocrisy. Now the fruit of righteousness is sown in peace by those who make peace." (Jas 3:13-18 NKJV)

You see, there are two types of wisdom and all things are built by one or the other. James calls the wisdom that doesn't descend from above as earthly wisdom and says that it is sensual and demonic. The other wisdom through which we are to build is the wisdom of God. Solomon was the king of peace who built Israel's kingdom through wisdom from God. This foreshadows the earth coming under the reign of Jesus, the prince of peace, where everything is a manifestation of the wisdom of God. This you could call the gates of heaven. We are called to extend the government of heaven through building by the wisdom of God. You could say that the gates of heaven will overcome the gates of hell here on earth.

Jesus reconciled all creation to God when He made peace through the cross. Through the gospel we administer this reconciliation. This is being a peacemaker. The gospel must bring people into obedience to heavenly wisdom; it must bring people into divine order. The gospel must be proclaimed in doctrines that accord with godliness; otherwise, it is useless. It must bring manifestations of heavenly wisdom; otherwise, it will create forms of religion without power. Such religion ultimately results in self-centered lovers of pleasure. The gospel is the power of God for salvation and it delivers people from the kingdom built by human wisdom and establishes people in the wisdom of God. The gospel brings forth the church where Jesus Christ is Lord and His kingdom is in manifestation.

Think a little about this salvation for a moment. When Adam and Eve were put in the garden, they were in the kingdom of God on the earth. Everything operated through spiritual power rather soul power. Adam had to take care of the whole garden, yet he never broke a sweat doing it because sweat came as part of the curse of sin. The earth brought forth blessing freely and in abundance. Everything was in harmony with the will of God. God gave the dominion of earth to Adam, and he was to govern it as he was under obedience to the government of God. Therefore, it would be a manifestation of the government of God. When Adam sinned, he gave the dominion of the earth to the devil. From that point creation began to be conformed into the image of sin.

From the moment Sin entered the world, God immediately began to deal with it. He would not let sin take captive those whom He loves. God in His mercy promised Adam and Eve in Gen 3:15 that He would restore man to paradise and destroy all of the works of the devil. The kingdom of God became a promise in the old covenant which became a reality in the new. That promise is being worked out in history. Around that promise God raised up a covenant people who were his chosen people to bring forth that promise. They were a people among whom God dwelt on the grounds of the atonement, yet they were not yet born again. They were a peculiar people among the whole earth because they were the only ones whom God dwelt with. While Israel was the covenant people of God, they were still under the law of sin and death.

The kingdom of God was in captivity from the time of Adam until Christ. They were still in bondage to the flesh until the messiah came. Everything about them was a testimony of Jesus to come. All of the glorious things that happened in their life were just shadows of the age that came when Jesus the Messiah cleansed the heavens and the earth by His blood!

Bondage to the flesh is the kingdom of sin and death. Where Jesus is Lord, life in the Spirit is the new law. After Adam sinned, he quit operating under the law of the spirit and instead operated by the works of the flesh. Soul power is doing things in the power of the flesh. It means doing things by human wisdom and strength. Notice that Galatians 5 refers to the works of the flesh and the fruit of the spirit. This is how these two realms operate. One is built by work and the other is simply a fruit of the spirit. There is incredible power in the soul, and it is able to do incredible things, but it can only go so far. The sorcerers in Egypt were able to imitate the signs that Moses worked, but only to a limit. There is a limit to the power of the soul. Even more, anything that is birthed by it will eventually wither and die. It cannot endure forever.

There were two trees with two different seeds in the garden. One speaks of spiritual power and the other of soul power. There are two kingdoms operating upon the earth until the final harvest.

"Now the whole earth had one language and one speech. And it came to pass, as they journeyed from the east, that they found a plain in the land of Shinar, and they dwelt there. Then they said to one another, "Come, let us make bricks and bake them thoroughly." They had brick for stone, and they had asphalt for mortar. And they said, "Come, let us build ourselves a city, and a tower whose top is in the heavens; let us make a name for ourselves, lest we be scattered abroad over the face of the whole earth."" (Ge 11:1-4 NKJV)

Here we see that man united himself in soulish wisdom and power in order to counterfeit the dominion of the spirit. God in His rich mercy comes and divides the languages, and their work comes to nothing. Soulish unity governed by fear is still the direction that the kingdom of darkness is striving for, but in the end it will come to nothing. Scripture links the tower of Babel to Babylon, and Babylon becomes a symbol for the kingdom which is built and governed by fear through soul power. It is a symbol for the kingdom built by the wisdom and power of men rather than by the wisdom and power of God. It is the kingdom that keeps people in bondage through the fear of death. The people are referred to as those who all their lives were subject to the fear of death. This is more than just physical death, it is the fear of being rejected, ridiculed, losing that which you hold dear, fear of sickness, poverty, fear of having your life be meaningless. It pertains to death in every way, shape and form.

The opposite of the kingdom of fear is the kingdom of love. Many people do not realize it but the opposite of love is not hate. They are actually two sides of the same coin. I love justice and hate injustice. I love freedom and hate oppression. I love righteousness and hate sin. The opposite of love is fear. The kingdom of God is a kingdom governed by love. Scripture tells us that perfect love casts out fear, and that is exactly what is taking place as the kingdom of God is growing on the earth today. It is not human love, a love that always has a hook of selfishness. It is the very love that God has in Himself. It is love that gives with no regard to self. This is the kingdom of light and life, of Jesus Christ.

> "After these things I saw another angel coming down from heaven, having great authority, and the earth was illuminated with his glory. And he cried mightily with a loud voice, saying, "Babylon the great is fallen, is fallen, and has become a dwelling place of demons, a prison for every foul spirit, and a cage for every unclean and hated bird! For all the nations have drunk of the wine of the wrath of her fornication, the kings of the earth have committed fornication with her, and the merchants of the earth have become rich through the abundance of her luxury." And I heard another voice from heaven saying, "Come out of her, my people, lest you share in her sins, and lest you receive of her plagues." (Re 18:1-4 NKJV)

Babylon will fall. It is written, and so it shall come to pass. Here the people of God are called to come out of her lest they share of her plagues. The book of Zechariah was written in a time when Babylon had already fallen to the Persians, yet listen to this prophesy.

> ""Up, up! Flee from the land of the north,"
> says the Lord; "for I have spread you abroad
> like the four winds of heaven," says the Lord.
> "Up, Zion! Escape, you who dwell with the
> daughter of Babylon."" (Zec 2:6-7 NKJV)

God is telling His people to flee from Babylon and come home to Jerusalem. Get out of the flesh and into the spirit. He tells them to escape because destruction is coming upon Babylon, and all who are part of her will share in her destruction. This is a call to those who weren't part of the remnant who returned from captivity and rebuilt the temple. It is directed to the people who chose to remain in captivity. Now that the temple is rebuilt, Babylon will be destroyed. Once the temple is rebuilt, and the presence and glory of God is manifested in His people, when Christians come to maturity, and we celebrate the feast of tabernacles, Babylon will be destroyed. The gates of hell shall not prevail.

The biblical strategy to deliver people from the house of bondage is to build a house of liberty for them to come to. There is nothing more powerful to bring people out of bondage and into the life of Christ than a church that has real spiritual life. The best way to win the lost, to see Christians come to maturity, for the kingdom of God to be extended is for Christians to be knit together with others who walk in real spiritual life. If people are going to come out of bondage, they need somewhere to come to. My counsel to people who are seeking God is to run with people who know God: people who are alive in the Spirit and growing with Christ, people who have real life in the spirit.

There is a call to the people of God to get out of Babylon. She is a harlot. She may appear to be very successful, but she is a harlot. She may appear to be very pleasing and desirable to the flesh but she is a harlot. She may bring you the praise and adoration of men but she is a harlot. She will be destroyed. She will be destroyed as God's ambassadors go into all the world and bring it into the obedience of Christ. She will be destroyed when every part of life is brought into the obedience of Christ and is governed by love. We cannot build the church of Jesus Christ using the wisdom and power of men. That simply grows Babylon. It must be built in the wisdom and power of God. This is the kingdom of God that was preached and manifested first in Jesus and then in the first generation apostles. This must be the way we build God's house.

"Then the seventy returned with joy, saying, "Lord, even the demons are subject to us in Your name." And He said to them, "I saw Satan fall like lightning from heaven. Behold, I give you the authority to trample on serpents and scorpions, and over all the power of the enemy, and nothing shall by any means hurt you. Nevertheless do not rejoice in this, that the spirits are subject to you, but rather rejoice because your names are written in heaven.'"" (Lk 10:17-20 NKJV)

Jesus sent the seventy disciples out under His anointing, not their anointing. The manifestation and demonstration of the Kingdom of God on earth was the reason Jesus proclaimed that He saw satan fall like lightning from heaven. When the kingdom of God is in manifestation it destroys the works of the devil. Jesus came for the purpose of destroying the works of the devil. He has already done it and it is being worked out on earth by His church. He has given His church authority over all the power of the enemy, and it will be manifested upon the earth.

These seventy disciples went out under Jesus' anointing and came back rejoicing because they healed the sick and cast out devils. They were very excited about this. Jesus tells them not to rejoice over this but that their names are written in the Lambs book of life. Even here Jesus is guarding them from falling into the flesh. Set your eyes right, and your whole body will be filled with light. If you start thinking you're great or that you have great power you will end up disconnecting from the life and power of Christ. He wants us to plug into His power, not to become disconnected from it.

The bottom line is that man is already seated in heavenly places far above all principality, power, rule and dominion in Christ. Man is already restored to the spiritual life that was lost in the fall. It is already accomplished in Jesus, and we are full partakers of it in Christ. It is the ministry of the church to bring agreement between heaven and earth. We need to use the keys of the kingdom of God and reveal the life that is already ours in Jesus upon the earth. This happens as we see Him. When we see Him by revelation we become like Him and manifest His life on the earth. It is His life that will destroys the works of the devil.

> "For we do not wrestle against flesh and blood, but against principalities, against powers, against the rulers of the darkness of this age, against spiritual hosts of wickedness in the heavenly places." (Eph 6:12 NKJV)

It is absolutely beautiful when you think about it. There are wicked spiritual princes and rulers who have ruled over the minds and lives of men for ages, and now they are being cast down. Their strongholds are being destroyed. Their gates are being demolished, and they are powerless to stop it. They have kept men in bondage through wicked works just as the Egyptians tried to oppress Israel through wicked works but now their kingdom is being brought to nothing. Jesus came as the mighty deliverer, and He is delivering the whole world through His body the church. We have the incredible privilege to be a part of this liberation of slaves through the ministry of reconciliation.

"For though we walk in the flesh, we do not war according to the flesh. For the weapons of our warfare are not carnal but mighty in God for pulling down strongholds, casting down arguments and every high thing that exalts itself against the knowledge of God, bringing every thought into captivity to the obedience of Christ, and being ready to punish all disobedience when your obedience is fulfilled." (2 Co 10:3-6 NKJV)

Everything that is disobedient to Christ will be destroyed, once our obedience if fulfilled. We overcome principalities when we are obedient to the kingdom of God. The battlefields where we often win the greatest victories are in the common contexts of life. Wherever there is the influence of the kingdom of darkness (if we are free from it through Christ) we will destroy it. If the stronghold is depression, and we are filled with joy in His presence, we begin to overthrow the enemy's throne. If the stronghold is discouragement we overthrow it with hope. Just like the battle in the Garden was over whether men chose to believe God or Satan, the same thing is true today. If we believe the lies of the enemy it will empower the darkness and carnal wisdom will be manifested. Everything we believe that is contrary to the truth of God's Word restricts our spiritual life. When we believe the truth of God's word it sets us free, and when we are liberated we shall free others. We can literally be conformed into the image of Christ. We are transformed, formed again through the renewing of our mind by the Word of God.

> "Through Him we have received grace and apostleship for obedience to the faith among all nations for His name," (Ro 1:5 NKJV)

There is power to bring the nations into the obedience of the faith. We are called to disciple nations, to bring them into the Peace of God. Biblical peace refers to wholeness and not simply the cessation of war. It is the cessation of everything that robs people of life. Biblical peace means to bring the order of heaven into a situation. This authority to disciple nations is the ability to heal and deliver the nations from bondage to the kingdom of darkness. This is the great call and ministry of the church.

Imagine a scale where the very top is heaven and the very bottom is hell. Everything in between heaven and hell represents earth. A person's life, our circumstances, our families, our work place, our communities, our nations can be located somewhere within this spectrum. Everything on earth has the potential to become more a manifestation of heaven or hell. Discipleship is the process of moving things into conformity with God's will which manifests heaven on earth. A person may be living almost in hell, but when they receive Jesus and start walking with him, their lives become transformed. He is the way to heaven. Just as the church is called to make disciples of people, we are also called to disciple nations, to move them more and more to a manifestation of the government of God.

How do we personally engage such a work? We do it by being obedient to the life of Christ. How do we do that? As we see Jesus we become like Him. Where did that take place? In the wilderness. The good news is that many will come forth in maturity and even creation itself will be liberated from bondage to corruption through the glorious liberty of the sons of God. The church has had its religious new year, and we are about to experience the civil new year where the government of God will be manifested in power.

The Mountain Church

—w—

"Now it shall come to pass in the latter days
That the mountain of the LORD's house Shall
be established on the top of the mountains,
And shall be exalted above the hills; And
peoples shall flow to it. Many nations shall
come and say, "Come, and let us go up to the
mountain of the LORD, To the house of the God
of Jacob; He will teach us His ways, And we
shall walk in His paths." For out of Zion the
law shall go forth, And the word of the LORD
from Jerusalem." (Mic 4:1-2 NKJV)

Mountains carry very important symbolism in
the Bible. They often represent governments
and power structures. Micah prophesies that in the
last days the mountain of the Lord's house shall be
over every other mountain and hill. This suggests
that in the lasts days the government of God will be
established over all of the earth. The mountain that
will rule over all the earth is mount Zion. Zion is
where the temple and the palace are, and therefore

represents the kingship and the priesthood. In the old covenant these two were separate from each other. In the new covenant the two become one, because the separation between God and man is torn down. Now the kingdom of God can actually reign upon the earth. It establishes God's law among men. It is the law of the Spirit. It delivers people from sin and empowers them to walk in love.

God reigns upon the earth from His throne. His throne is in the midst of His temple. The place where this is located in scripture is mount Zion. God's temple must never be arbitrarily built.

"And see to it that you make *them* according to the pattern which was shown you on the mountain." (Ex 25:40 NKJV)

Before Moses began the work of building the temple, he was taken up on Mt. Sinai and was shown the pattern for the temple. The temple that he built was not built according to the plans, purposes or architecture of men but was built according to the divine pattern. Just as the tabernacle in the old covenant was built according to the divine patter, so is the temple that is being built in the new covenant. The pattern for the new covenant is seen in the life of Jesus and the Acts of the Apostles.

What is interesting is that the temple that was on Mount Zion was not the same temple that was built by Moses; it was the temple that was built by Solomon according to the directions that David received from

God. This suggests that the kingdom of God continually advances in the earth.

> ""All *this,*" *said David,* "the Lord made me understand in writing, by *His* hand upon me, all the works of these plans."" (1 Ch 28:19 NKJV)

Today we refer to Israelites as Jews. Jerusalem, and especially Mount Zion with the palace and temple became the focal point of Israel. It was the temple on mount Zion that God chose for His dwelling place.

> ""But you shall seek the place where the LORD your God chooses, out of all your tribes, to put His name for His dwelling place; and there you shall go." (Dt 12:5 NKJV)

Considering the incredible significance of Mount Zion, it is surprising that it was occupied by Canaanites for approximately 240 years after Israel took possession of the Promised Land. Israel did not take possession of it until David came into his kingship. This demonstrates how the church of Israel came into their inheritance when they were mature. It happened as God's redemptive plan unfolded upon the earth.

> "David *was* thirty years old when he began to reign, *and* he reigned forty years. In Hebron he reigned over Judah seven years and six months, and in Jerusalem he reigned thirty-

three years over all Israel and Judah. And the king and his men went to Jerusalem against the Jebusites, the inhabitants of the land, who spoke to David, saying, "You shall not come in here; but the blind and the lame will repel you," thinking, "David cannot come in here." Nevertheless David took the stronghold of Zion (that *is,* the City of David)." (2 Sa 5:4-7 NKJV)

All of this seems to speak about where we are at with the kingdom of God in the church of Jesus Christ. It has been about 2000 years since the church was formed and now we are about to see the church come to mount Zion. We are about to see the church come into her destiny and see the manifestation of the kingdom of God.

There are three basic anointings in scripture: that of the prophet, the king and the priest. While there were prophets and priests in Israel long before there was a king, so has it been in the church. The church is about to see the anointing of spiritual kingship be restored to the church. It is the same anointing that we saw in the life and ministry of Jesus and the first apostles. It was the manifestation of the kingdom of God.

Let us think for a moment about the conversion of Saul. He was a persecutor of the church of Jesus. He had a reputation among the Jews, carnal authority granted by men, and was very zealous to destroy the church. On his way to Damascus, with authority to wreak havoc on the church, he encountered Jesus.

How did he encounter Jesus? A light shined from heaven, he fell on his face, and he heard the Lord speak to him directly. Jesus actually gave him very specific directions about what he should do. After the Lord was done speaking to him, he discovered that the Lord had also blinded him. He was three days without food or water, and he had a prophetic vision that a man named Ananias would lay hands on him, and he would receive his sight. The next thing you know, Ananias showed up, gave him a word of knowledge, prophesied to him, laid hands on him and he received his sight. He got baptized in the Holy Spirit, and he got water baptized. What an incredible first week as a Christian. Why do you think he had such an incredible conversion? Some may think that it has to do with how important his calling was, and certainly there is truth in that, but I want to challenge us to ponder the possibility that it has much more to do with the level of light, life, and power being manifested in the Church.

Paul was persecuting the church just like Pharaoh persecuted Israel, but everything turned out for their growth. He saw the incredible manifestation of Jesus when Stephen was martyred. No, he didn't see the heavens opened, but he saw its reflection in how Stephen responded to the whole situation. I would also be willing to bet that Saul was the most prayed for man in the whole world at the time of His conversion, whether directly or indirectly through prayers that would get him tangled up in the middle of it all. As we continue to examine the life, light and power in the church at that time, we realize that such a conversion does not seem so unusual but quite usual. As a matter of fact, scripture later testifies about unusual miracles being worked by the hands of Paul (Saul also had his name changed to Paul.) When you read through the book of Acts and examine the litany of miracles, it is hard to imagine what unusual miracles might look like.

Going back to his conversion, you see that Ananias played an important role in it. What is interesting is that we know very little about Ananias. He appears to be just another run of the mill disciple of Jesus. Jesus spoke to him in a vision, and the Biblical record makes it seem like there is nothing unusual about this at all. Jesus gave Ananias very specific information on what he was to do, and He also gave him very specific information about what was going on with Saul. So what was Ananias' response? He argued with God because he was not sure it was a good idea to go and minister to Saul. God commanded him to go and he obeyed. What else is interesting about this whole encounter is that God told Ananias that Saul had already seen in a vision a man named Ananias coming and laying hands on him. Wow! God hadn't even told Ananias yet! He had people who could hear and obey. It is a good thing that He actually had people that He was lord over. In many contexts today such a conversion could never take place simply because there is no Ananias. Who is this Ananias anyway? I think he is just another average Joe disciple.

Going back to the analogy of climbing a mountain, I challenge that the church we saw in Jesus' ministry was reproduced in that first generation church. As generations of Christians passed on, the church started to decline until the time of the reformation. During the reformation, the church began being restored to that which it was at first. At every age and in every place it seems that people come into the church at the level of light and life that the church carries. Just think about all of the revivals of religion that have broken out all over the world throughout history. People came into and experienced the life of the people of God that was manifested in that time and place. They immediately became partakers of the common life manifested in the church. For example, whenever there has been an outbreak of Pentecost we find that baby Christians come in and immediately start experiencing the gifts of the spirit being ministered to them and through them. Such experiences produce wonderful testimonies. The reason that there was such spiritual life manifested in the church is because there were those there who were spiritually mature. It is absolutely necessary that we see people come to spiritual maturity in order for us to experience a similar Christianity as we see in the book of Acts.

I believe that the wilderness is the place where God brings people to maturity, but I also believe that the wilderness that one person goes through is radically different from the wilderness another one goes through. If we look carefully at the church in Acts we see that the very same church that had people who were spiritually mature was also filled with babies who were spiritually immature. These babes in Christ grew up in churches where there was an incredible amount of life and light. Their experiences of Christianity from day one of being born again would probably be radically different than many people who are Christians today. It doesn't mean that we have had less of a legitimate conversion, or that we have less of a commitment to Christ, it simply means that they were born into churches that had much more life and power and a much higher standard of Christian experience than many of us have had today. The good news is that the church is being revived!

Think for a moment about Elijah and Elisha. If you look at the Biblical record you will see that Elisha had a greater number of miracles. Notice what Elijah had to pay for his anointing and what Elisha had to pay for his. Elijah was surrounded by enemies and hardship and suffered greatly. Elisha was a friend of the king who received an inherited anointing from Elijah. (The double portion Elisha received from Elijah signifies he inherited from Elijah the anointing as though he was Elijah's first born son.) Elijah truly was a great mountain climber. Very few have revived the level of true religion as Elijah did. I think one of the greatest honors of Elijah's life and ministry is Elisha. He was able to cause his son in the Lord to go above and beyond where he lived. Elisha was not forced to start over from scratch but was able to continue where Elijah left off. This Elisha became an heir of Elijah's ministry.

Look at Moses and Joshua. Think about all that Moses had to go through to come to maturity. He was in the wilderness of Midian tending sheep. He had very little experience with the kingdom of

God. Joshua, on the other hand, saw what God did through Moses in bringing Israel out of Egypt. He saw the cloud by day and pillar by night. He ate the manna from heaven. He spent long hours in the tent of meeting. His wilderness looked radically different from that of Moses because he was an heir of his spiritual father's ministry.

Think of David and Solomon. Think of all that David had to go through to come into his kingdom and then think of Solomon. He was an heir of his father's ministry. As I mentioned earlier, when the seventy were sent out by Jesus they were ministering under His anointing and had no anointing of their own. Jesus' disciples actually came to maturity under His wonderful ministry. They were heirs of their spiritual father's ministry. Today God wants to reproduce the exact same life in us.

Ponder the fruit of Jesus' ministry in the first generation church. (They were the first generation of born again believers from Jesus.) At the day of Pentecost we see that tongues of fire rest upon them and they begin speaking in tongues. The people who are gathered from around the world to Jerusalem for the feast of Pentecost all hear them praising God in their native languages. This is the reversal of the curse. It is the opposite of what happened at the tower of Babel. It is a sign that Jesus is on the throne and that dominion is restored through the son of man to the sons of God. Man is restored to his position lost from the fall. Notice how it is the Spirit that restores dominion and it is the Spirit that is the source of unity. In the Spirit everyone is united in Christ. In the flesh everyone is divided. It is the sign that there is a changing of rulers and a changing of the law. Man is no longer under the law of sin and death but in Christ is under the law of the Spirit of life. It is the sign that the curse has been destroyed and the way to the tree of life is open. That miracle of speaking in tongues is an amazing proclamation of Biblical truth!

What happens? Many are born again as sons of God. The kingdom of God grows and its borders are extended. These Christians were first generation heirs of Jesus' ministry. Their church was a continuation of Jesus' church in the gospels. It was a manifestation of heavenly government here on earth.

"And through the hands of the apostles many signs and wonders were done among the people. And they were all with one accord in Solomon's Porch. Yet none of the rest dared join them, but the people esteemed them highly. And believers were increasingly added to the Lord, multitudes of both men and women, so that they brought the sick out into the streets and laid them on beds and couches, that at least the shadow of Peter passing by might fall on some of them. Also a multitude gathered from the surrounding cities to Jerusalem, bringing sick people and those who were tormented by unclean spirits, and they were all healed." (Ac 5:12-16 NKJV)

It is absolutely wonderful. Many signs and wonders were worked through the hands of the apostles, yet people were afraid to join them. Never the less, multitudes were born again. Sounds funny doesn't it? People were afraid of what was going on, yet they esteemed the Christians highly, but they didn't want to identify with them. Despite all that God kept birthing children. It is hilarious: people didn't want to join them, but if they had someone sick they would put them out on the streets because the presence of the kingdom of God was so powerful that Peter's shadow would heal them. Multitudes from the surrounding cities brought the demon possessed and the sick, and they were all healed. Wow! Please tell me what unusual miracles look like because I am quite amazed by usual ones. I can't see how this looks any different than the ministry of Jesus himself. Think about growing up in such a church. Maybe Jesus was so good at making disciples that He perfectly reproduced himself in that first batch.

The question we need to ask ourselves is: why are such things recorded for us in the book of Acts? Are they simply stories to amaze us with what God did in those days or are they given for our instruction and edification so that we see what God will do in us today? Do we believe that it is possible for us to experience the very same Christianity? I think an even better question is: does the Biblical record prove that such a reproduction of the life of Christ is God's agenda for the Church until the end of time?

""Most assuredly, I say to you, he who believes in Me, the works that I do he will do also; and greater works than these he will do, because I go to My Father." (Jn 14:12 NKJV)

Such statements hold out before us the possibility of a religion that few have dared to believe. No wonder Jesus saw satan fall like lightning. There is no way that satan's kingdom can continue in the midst of the kingdom of God. No wonder there were such incredible persecutions of those first believers. When satan showed Jesus all the kingdoms of the earth and offered them to Jesus if he would bow down and worship him, it was a real temptation because the devil actually ruled over all of those kingdoms. He was able to have his will done in them. He was able to cause them to crucify Jesus, and as if he didn't learn the first time he continued to crucify God's sons. Yet the kingdom kept growing. What else could he do? Maybe Balaam had some good ideas. Lead the church astray to play the harlot. Get them to take foreign wives. Seduce them with doctrines of devils. Cause them to compromise. Pollute the temple. The devil had to try something or it would all be over. Instead of persecution he tried seduction. He seduced the church with the wisdom and power of Egypt. Such doctrines of devils oppress the sons of God so that they remain babies, so that they never come to maturity. This results in Christians who, although they are heirs, they appear no different than slaves of sin. The good news is that every tactic of the devil intended to destroy the church will ultimately lead to her establishment and exaltation. When the enemy intends for evil, God always overrides for good.

Know for certain that God will complete the work He began in the church. The sons of God will come to maturity. The church is coming out of the wilderness, and every work of the devil will be destroyed under her feet.

> "Assuredly, I say to you, there are some standing here who shall not taste death till they see the Son of Man coming in His kingdom.""" (Mt 16:28 NKJV)

> "And He said to them, "Assuredly, I say to you that there are some standing here who will not taste death till they see the kingdom of God present with power.""" (Mk 9:1 NKJV)

The great proclamation of Jesus is that the kingdom of God is at hand. What he is basically saying is that the government of God is present in His life and ministry. Jesus promises that some of those who were His disciples would see the kingdom present with power. When did that happen? At the day of Pentecost! There were many in the world that did not see the kingdom of God present in Jesus because they were geographically disconnected from it. The same thing was true at the day of Pentecost. Many in the world that day never saw it. Many people who actually saw Jesus in the days of His flesh never saw the kingdom present in power. They could not recognize it even in Jesus. Even though it was in their midst, they were blind and could not see it. The same thing was true at Pentecost, and the same thing has been true throughout all history, yet ever since the day of Pentecost the kingdom of God has been present with power. There have been various levels of its manifestation, but it has always been present. In the days when Elijah was raised up, it appeared to him that he was the only one left who served the Lord. Actually there were 7000 left, but even Elijah didn't know it. The manifestation of God's kingdom had become so restricted that in many ways it appeared gone, yet God has never let the light go out.

The dark ages were truly spiritually dark, but if we look closely we can still find the record of the remnant. We can still find outposts of the kingdom of God. When everything appeared like the kingdom would be lost, something began to happen. In one of the darkest hours of history, a glorious light dawned. Today we call it the reformation. A fire was lit and it still is growing. What began as a discovery of justification by faith is now bringing us to a place where the people of God will come to maturity and be conformed into the image of Christ. The revelation of Jesus is growing in the earth. All things in history are speeding up toward the consummation of the promises of God. The birth pains are everywhere. The Sons of God are coming. Both seeds have been growing in the garden of the world; the day of harvest is quickly approaching. The Church is about to come out of the wilderness leaning on her beloved.

Even that first church at Jerusalem went through birth pangs. They had ideas of how the kingdom was going to work and God had different ideas. God wanted the gospel to go to all the world, but they would have been content with a Jewish thing. Look how God worked with Peter to get the gospel to Cornelius. Look how it made its way to Samaria. Look at the wisdom of God's ways. God used the persecution headed up by Saul to scatter the fire of Pentecost all over. Everywhere it went it destroyed the works of the devil with its fire. The devil tried to put it out, but all it did was spread. All the systems of Babylon are being destroyed by the fire of God. The fire of Pentecost is the presence of God. Man has come into communion with God because of the cross. This communion creates the kingdom of God on earth. God's presence is a consuming fire, a fire of love, which destroys all the works of the devil. It destroys the world systems built by sin. It destroys Babylon.

Later, this same Paul who scattered the church through persecution into gentile regions becomes the great apostle to the gentiles. His ministry among the gentiles will one day provoke the Jews to jealousy. It will reap a harvest among all of the nations of mature sons of God. Their manifestation in the word will lead to Israel's repentance. They will receive Jesus the messiah. It is promised in scriptures. God always fulfills His promises. Paul's ministry to the gentiles is fulfilling ancient prophesies that all of the treasures of the gentiles will be brought into the house of God. God's ways are truly amazing!

This is a small picture of Mountain climbing. It is the story of our lives and the story of the church. We keep breaking through into more and more revelation of Jesus, and the territory of the kingdom in our life and in the world is extended.

The life of Paul is very instructional for us. He had a glorious deliverance from Egypt just like Israel. Then he disappeared into the wilderness for about 10 years. He was not seen or heard from. This is a pattern that is played out time and time again. Many people have incredible experiences when they first come to know Jesus. It is like David slaying Goliath, leading the armies of Saul into victory and then suddenly he finds himself in the wilderness. Those first experiences are so critical for us in order to make it through the wilderness. If it wasn't for the wonder and glory of those first experiences we would probably not make it through the wilderness. They give us something to remember as God basically crushes the olive in the wilderness to get at the oil. In a sense such experiences are the seal and guarantee that He will get us through. That is what the book of acts is for the church. It is the seal and guarantee that He will bring us through into the Promised Land. Certainly our wildernesses are all different, and much of that has to do with the context we are in, but at the end of the day God will perfect the church just as He has promised. There is no way around it. Even those first generation Christians who grew up in Jesus' church had to go through the wilderness. You could almost say that the wilderness for the first disciples was from the time Jesus called them to the day of Pentecost. During that time the disciples died to every confidence they may have had in the flesh. In a very real way, Peter died the day he denied the Lord.

While Paul is in the wilderness, God initiates a kingdom outpost in Antioch. It was a wonderful manifestation of heaven. Because of the persecution that arose over Stephen, the gospel spread, but only to Jews. Then, here in Antioch the gospel breaks out among the gentiles. God is so invested in the thing that they start growing incredibly. The news of the gospel spreading made its way to Jerusalem and they sent Barnabas out to visit the churches that have been birthed. When he gets to Antioch he finds it is rapidly growing. By adding his ministry and anointing in the mix it really takes off. Because of its success, they need some help. Barnabas remembers Paul and goes to Tarsus and brings him to Antioch. They are there for about five years with a couple of journeys to Jerusalem thrown in. That Antioch church was a beautiful outpost of heaven. It tore down racial and social divisions in the Spirit of the Lord. There were wonderful gifts of the Spirit in operation. It was a stronghold of the kingdom of God. After about five years serving in that church, God sent Paul and Barnabas out as church planters. It took about 15 years from the time Paul was born again until he came into his calling as an apostle.

Paul as an apostle has the authority or spiritual ability to bring forth kingdom outposts. He certainly is an ambassador of heaven and an apostle of Jesus Christ called to manifest the kingdom of heaven on earth, but he is also a representative of the church in Antioch. That was the most complete representation of the kingdom of heaven he knew at the time, and that was the starting point for him to go out and reproduce that same life elsewhere in the world.

This is how reproduction works, we bring forth after our own kind. We cannot give what we haven't first received. This is why people who come to Christ in different churches have extremely different kingdom experiences. They partake of the common life of the church they know. The more we can add to the life of the churches, the greater the expression of the kingdom will be. This is why we need to give and receive the gift of God that He has entrusted to every one of us. This is why it is so critical that every member of the body of Christ fulfill the ministry which God has ordained for them.

Let us think about energy for a moment. There have always been sources of energy in the world, but as people have learned to harness them, it has brought forth all kinds of marvelous things. The power has always been here, but it was practically useless until men discovered how to use it. As people learned to tap into the power that has always been here, as we learned the laws that governed energy, and learned how to put it to work, it has revolutionized the whole world. That is no exaggeration. Just as people have discovered how to use the incredible power in the simple things around us like coal, oil, water, light and even atoms, so also when we discover all of what has been available in Christ and we learn the laws that govern it shall we see a wonderful revival of the kingdom of God on earth.

There is incredible power in the gospel of Jesus to take everything that is in heaven and reveal it on the earth. I believe that we are quickly approaching the time where God will cause the church to be all that He intends it to be. I believe if we look closely at what has happened in church history we will see that God has been moving us forward ever since the first kingdom rediscovery which was "we are saved by grace through faith apart from works according to scripture." That simple truth has significantly impacted every society on the earth, but it was just the beginning of the revival of the church that is simply the restoration of the very life Jesus has in Himself!

After justification by faith was restored, the church then discovered how to enter the inner courts, and the church celebrated Pentecost. All kinds of gifts of the spirit have operated around the world and have brought forth incredible blessings to every nation. If we look closely, we see that even the revivals of Wesley and Finney were of this nature. They were filled with the signs of Pentecost even if they used different terms or had less understanding of it than we do today. They often manifested more of Pentecost than many who teach about it today.

Right now we are at a time in history where we can expect the sons of God to be revealed upon the earth. When the church rediscovered justification by faith you could say we celebrated Passover. As the church discovered sanctification by faith you could say the church experienced Pentecost. Now we are about to see the people who have submitted to the Lord coming forth from the wilderness in maturity and we will then celebrate the feast of tabernacles.

We will see a civil year begin where the authority of the kingdom of God is in manifestation. It was all in the DNA we received when we were born again and it is now about to be revealed upon the earth. Spiritually, the church is about to take Jerusalem, and mount Zion will be established over all of the earth. It is all awaiting the revelation of the sons of God.

Kingdom Blue Prints

—◊◊◊—

Having an intellectual knowledge concerning where we are at spiritually is important, but even more important is to receive the revelation of the pattern through which we are to build the house of God. It seems to me that there are many people who love to get hyped up about things that sound exciting. The kingdom of God is not built on hype, but on obedience to Christ. There are many people who seem to be obsessed with seeing miracles and great manifestations of power. When I think of great miracle workers besides Jesus, I think about Peter and Paul. What is amazing is that most of their writings are not about how to work miracles, but how to make disciples and build the church.

> ""Then if anyone says to you, 'Look, here *is* the Christ!' or 'There!' do not believe *it*. For false christs and false prophets will rise and show great signs and wonders to deceive, if possible, even the elect. See, I have told you beforehand." (Mt 24:23-25 NKJV)

The word Christ besides referring to Jesus can also refer to the anointing. It is as though people in the last days will declare that God's anointing is in different places, but if the fruit does not line up with the Word of God it is illegitimate, not belonging to God. Even if there are amazing things happening, if it isn't according to the Word of God it is out of bounds. Even the works of the flesh can do some amazing things, never mind spiritual hosts of wickedness in heavenly places.

Often times, people will be encouraged to try different superstitious things to try to get the power of God working. Superstitious religious rituals are things that Jesus died to deliver us from. People still try barking up such trees, and when it continually falls short of Biblical Christianity, they assume they aren't trying hard enough. They should check with the scriptures to see if there is anything good in the tree they are convinced will bear fruit.

The blue prints for the church are all in scriptures. Looking at the birthday of the church, Pentecost, many people get excited about the tongues of fire and speaking so that everyone heard it in their own native language. Often times people speak of that day like it was a great party, and they wish they could reproduce it. What really excites me about that day is the fruit it bore. That day, about 3000 people who were dead in their sins were born again. Peter, who cowered with fear at Jesus' crucifixion, boldly preaches before men. While some accused them of being drunk, look at how soberly Peter addresses the people. Notice how this celebration of Pentecost, rather than being a substitute for scripture, was an enlightenment of it. Look how much of Peter's preaching reveals scriptures in the light of God's presence. This is prophetic preaching, and it was as though God himself was speaking through Peter to the people.

We need to see that the greatest miracle in the world is a disciple of Christ.

> "He (Jesus) was in the world, and the world was made through Him, and the world did not know Him. He came to His own, and His own did not receive Him. But as many as received Him, to them He gave the right to become children of God, to those who believe in His name: who were born, not of blood, nor of the will of the flesh, nor of the will of man, but of God." (Jn 1:10-13 NKJV)

Nothing is more spectacular than a child of Adam to become a child of God. Nothing is more important for humanity, but it will have little help to humanity unless that child of God grows to maturity.

The people who heard Peter preaching on the day of Pentecost were cut to the heart. They inquired what they must do to be saved. What is salvation? Is it not being saved from being ruled by sin and death and instead to be ruled by Christ? Is this not what discipleship is all about? Salvation is not a divine insurance policy for our afterlife; it is coming under the Lordship of Jesus now. This is what it means to be saved. Peter's answer to their inquiry is for them to repent and to be baptized. So often Christians think of baptism as the ritual, but the meaning of baptism is to come into the life of something. Essentially, Peter told the people to repent and come into the life of disciples. It was a call to join the church. People are not born again by the ritual of baptism or by joining a church; they are born again by faith in Jesus. Yet the call to the people was more than a call to be born again, it was a call to become a disciple of Jesus. Christians today need to understand this and get past simply trying to get people to say a "sinner's prayer." Those who heard Peter preach that day became disciples, and Acts records what the new emphasis of their lives became.

> "Then those who gladly received his word were baptized; and that day about three thousand souls were added *to them.* And they continued steadfastly in the apostles' doctrine and fellowship, in the breaking of bread, and in prayers. Then fear came upon every soul, and many wonders and signs were done through the apostles. Now all who believed were together, and had all things in common, and sold their possessions and goods, and divided them among all, as anyone had need. So continuing daily with one accord in the temple, and breaking bread from house to house, they ate their food with gladness and simplicity of heart, praising God and having favor with all the people. And the Lord added to the church daily those who were being saved." (Ac 2:41-47 NKJV)

This is the pattern for church which causes the kingdom of God to be manifested. The emphasis is not on the miracles, but on people's daily normal lives. It is how people live daily that provides the context for the power of God to be manifested.

The very next story recorded in Acts is of Peter and John going to the temple for the time of prayer, which we see from the above scripture, was their daily routine. On their way into the temple they heal a man who had been lame since birth. Peter, when he preaches to the crowd that is drawn because of the miracle tells us that it took place through faith in Jesus.

> "And His name, through faith in His name, has made this man strong, whom you see and know. Yes, the faith which *comes* through Him has given him this perfect soundness in the presence of you all." (Ac 3:16 NKJV)

What I love about this story is not only the things that are recorded, but also the things that weren't. Whose faith is Peter referring to? His, or the man who was healed? I would say it was both of their faith.

We were told that the lame man was laid daily at the temple. It is possible that Peter and John passed him many times on their way to prayer and he was never healed. It is also possible that he was there when Jesus visited the temple. Why did he not get healed earlier? I suggest that he was not yet ripe for harvest.

"And He said, "The kingdom of God is as if a man should scatter seed on the ground, and should sleep by night and rise by day, and the seed should sprout and grow, he himself does not know how. For the earth yields crops by itself: first the blade, then the head, after that the full grain in the head. But when the grain ripens, immediately he puts in the sickle, because the harvest has come."" (Mk 4:26-29 NKJV)

I bet that he had heard the testimony of Jesus, probably during the time of Jesus' public ministry. Since the word of what happened through His ministry spread abroad, it likely would have caught the ear of a lame man at the temple. I doubt that the first time the lame man heard the name of Jesus was the day Peter healed him. It probably took more time for the seed of the gospel to grow in him until it was ripe for harvest.

The other side of the story is the faith of Peter. He acted in obedience to Christ when he healed the lame man. Often, when people start speaking about healing or deliverance, it sounds like they think that we should be able to go and heal anybody at any time. Well, that isn't the Biblical pattern. Neither Jesus nor the apostles ever healed this man until he was ripe for harvest.

What is wonderful is that Peter knew what to do. He must have received directions from the Lord. Maybe he received it during in a vision, like he will later concerning Cornelius. Maybe he heard the Holy

Spirit speak to him when he arrived at the temple. We do not know how he got the revelation, but the point is that He must have received the revelation of what to do, and then acted in obedience, just like Ananias did for Paul.

> "Then Jesus answered and said to them, "Most assuredly, I say to you, the Son can do nothing of Himself, but what He sees the Father do; for whatever He does, the Son also does in like manner." (Jn 5:19 NKJV)

It appears to me that the apostles are continuing the ministry of Jesus. The context where all the great miracles of the book of Acts take place is people living out a life of biblical discipleship. Therefore I conclude that the way we go about seeking the manifestation of the kingdom of God is through seeing people conform their lives to biblical discipleship.

River of Life

—⟪⟫—

"And he showed me a pure river of water of life, clear as crystal, proceeding from the throne of God and of the Lamb. In the middle of its street, and on either side of the river, was the tree of life, which bore twelve fruits, each tree yielding its fruit every month. The leaves of the tree were for the healing of the nations. And there shall be no more curse, but the throne of God and of the Lamb shall be in it, and His servants shall serve Him. They shall see His face, and His name shall be on their foreheads." (Re 22:1-4 NKJV)

John saw these things because they are actually already accomplished in heaven. There is no way of it changing. I do believe that they look forward to the very end, but there is much instruction to be taken from them because they show you things that are true in heaven.

First there is a river of life that proceeds from the throne of God and of the lamb. Wherever Jesus is Lord, wherever His rule is manifested, there is a river of life that proceeds from His throne. It is true in every area of our life, wherever we submit to the Lordship of Jesus it causes a river of life to flow. Scripture teaches us that the life is in the blood. In a very real sense the river is the river of the life of Christ. When we were born again, we received that life. We became partakers of His blood. Yet, there is no river of life flowing out from the temple unless Jesus is actually on the throne. Wherever we fail to submit to His lordship, it actually blocks the flow of life out of the temple to the world.

Next, we see that on either side of the river of life, the tree of life grows. This speaks of growing things that are of the Spirit. The tree bears the fruit of the Spirit, and it constantly yields its fruit. It tangibly manifests the life that is in the blood of Jesus. This is contrary to what is manifested through the works of the flesh. The leaves are for the healing of the nations. From this we see a pattern. Wherever the life of Christ flows from the temple it will cause things to grow that will manifest the wisdom of heaven and will bring healing to the nations. When Jesus is manifested as Lord in the church it will cause the garden of God to grow on earth. This is why we must come to maturity. The hope for all the nations is in the manifestation of God's government. All of creation is to be reconciled through the cross, and that includes every sphere of life. As people operate in the Spirit rather than the flesh, when they are ruled by love rather than fear, when they walk in the power of God that empowers them to walk in love, it causes heaven to be revealed on earth. All the nations of the earth shall be blessed, but ironically this perspective depends on where you are sitting. If you are sitting with the righteous you see that this life is healing the nations. If you are sitting with the wicked it appears that this life is destroying the world because it destroys the rule of sin and death that people have used to make themselves rich at the expense of others. This is judgment; God is ruling in favor of righteousness and against wickedness.

Wherever the throne of God is the curse is no more. It is absolutely wonderful. Wherever we submit to the government of God the works of the devil are destroyed. Wherever the throne of God is, people serve the law of love, they see God, and His very character and nature is revealed in them. What an incredible picture of spiritual truth that has incredible significance for us today. Every area of life in the world that comes under the dominion of Jesus Christ, or in other words the dominion of love, will actually cause the blessings of God to be manifested on the earth. It all has to do with us bearing the fruit of the Spirit rather than operating in the works of the flesh. It all has to do with us being crucified with Christ so that His life may be manifested to us, in us and through us.

"On the last day, that great day of the feast, Jesus stood and cried out, saying, "If anyone thirsts, let him come to Me and drink. He who believes in Me, as the Scripture has said, out of his heart will flow rivers of living water." But this He spoke concerning the Spirit, whom those believing in Him would receive; for the Holy Spirit was not yet given, because Jesus was not yet glorified." (Jn 7:37-39 NKJV)

Here we see that Jesus testifies of this truth and the only date that He puts it off until is the day of Pentecost. All who believe in Jesus will have His life flow forth from them. These are the rivers of living water that we just read about. Notice that He connects the rivers flowing with those who believe. This is how we operate in the realm of the Spirit; it is by the law of faith. It is not through the works of the flesh.

"Then they said to Him, "What shall we do, that we may work the works of God?" Jesus answered and said to them, "This is the work of God, that you believe in Him whom He sent."" (Jn 6:28-29 NKJV)

The works of God are by the spirit and not the flesh. They operate in the realm of faith. All the works we see in the gospels and greater we will do because Jesus went to the father. How are they done? By the works of the law or through the hearing of faith?

"Then Jesus said to those Jews who believed Him, "If you abide in My word, you are My disciples indeed. And you shall know the truth, and the truth shall make you free."" (Jn 8:31-32 NKJV)

We are disciples of Jesus through abiding in His word. Through abiding in His word we shall know the truth, and it shall set us free. This is how the kingdom of God works. Jesus and the Word are one. He is the Word in flesh. When we know the Word, we will know the truth and the truth shall set us free from everything that pertains to the kingdom of darkness. In other words, we will know Jesus and our knowledge of Him will set us free. It is not the knowledge about him but the fellowship and communion with Him that will set us free. This takes us right back to the rock upon which the church is built. We will know him by revelation. It is a relational knowledge of Jesus. Such fellowship with Jesus will cause us to walk in obedience to the kingdom of His love rather than the kingdom of sin and death.

There is something else I want us to see about the river of life and the rivers of living water. We mentioned earlier that the life is in the blood so it is the ministry of the blood of Jesus. Also notice that we received that life when we were born again.

"Having been born again, not of corruptible seed but incorruptible, through the word of God which lives and abides forever," (1 Pe 1:23 NKJV)

The gospel of John tells us that Jesus is the Word of God who dwelt among us. Therefore, rivers of living water are also connected to rivers of the living Word of God. Now look at Ephesians.

"Husbands, love your wives, just as Christ also loved the church and gave Himself for her, that He might sanctify and cleanse her with the washing of water by the word, that He might present her to Himself a glorious church, not having spot or wrinkle or any such thing, but that she should be holy and without blemish." (Eph 5:25-27 NKJV)

If we look closely at Ephesians, Paul is calling us to walk in kingdom obedience, which is walking in love in real life. The word that Paul uses is that husbands are to "agape" their wives. This word for love is a word that refers to the very life of God, who is agape. This type of love is a new love that is only available in the new covenant. It is the very love that is in God, and it is the very love that is to rule and govern the world. This same love sanctifies the church. Through the washing of water by the Word, God's people become conformed into His image. The living Word of God cleanses the church and presents her without spot or wrinkle. It happens as we believe what God says rather than everything that speaks contrary. This is what cleanses the church. Jesus is coming for a pure spotless bride.

""For this reason a man shall leave his father and mother and be joined to his wife, and the two shall become one flesh." This is a great mystery, but I speak concerning Christ and the church." (Eph 5:31-32 NKJV)

Paul talks about a man and a woman becoming one flesh and he sees in this the relationship between Christ and the church. What it actually refers to is the marriage of heaven and earth. It is God's will being done on earth as it is in heaven. The keys of the kingdom in operation bring this to pass. It is seeing Jesus and becoming like Him and having His life manifested in our mortal, death-doomed bodies.

Look at Stephen for a moment. He was the first martyr, a witness of the Lord. The word we know today as martyr comes from the Greek cognate which is translated "to be a witness." Because so many witnesses of the Lord died for their testimony, the word came to refer to someone who dies for their testimony. Yet the word also had connections to prophets because they testified the living word of God to the people. We are a prophetic people who, through word and deed, testify about Jesus. We speak the living Word of God and it causes Christ's life to become manifested in our flesh. We speak and believe the Word of God and it causes the life of Christ to be revealed to us, in us and through us.

Now back to Stephen, the first martyr. He wasn't the first witness because the disciples witnessed very powerfully from the day of Pentecost. Yet he was the first martyr. He was a deacon in the church. The apostles saw that the power of God was waning in their ministry because they were getting too busy, so they ordained deacons to help carry the load. They chose men with a good reputation, full of wisdom and the Holy Spirit. Stephen was one of those men. I'm not sure of the exact details of his job, but one thing I know is that it put him in the middle of bickering women. Sound like a fun place to be? What else do we know about him? We know that he was full of faith and the power of the Holy Spirit and that he worked great signs and wonders among the people. We also know that he preached in the power of the Spirit. He looks a lot like Jesus doesn't he? Many people who are put into the fire of bickering people would become bitter because of it. In Stephen it worked something beautiful; he just grew in grace and love. He grew more and more like Jesus because he kept fellowship with the Word. As he continued to see Jesus he continued to become like him and have Jesus' life manifested in his mortal body until the two became one. Even at his death he testified that he saw Jesus and in seeing him he became like him crying "Father forgive them."

It was continual fellowship with the Word or Jesus that caused Stephen to become conformed to the image of Christ. Think for a minute: if he would have decided to have fellowship with darkness when he was thrown into the middle of bickering women, his testimony would have been different. He would no longer have been a witness of Christ. He would have become conformed to darkness and would have been a witness of the kingdom of darkness. He may have proclaimed that he had fellowship with the light, but the fact that he would be walking in darkness would have testified otherwise. He would have lost his saltiness. Praise God that Stephen kept his eyes fixed on Jesus and his whole body was filled with light.

I love the heroes of faith in Hebrews 11 but not the cowards of Hebrews 14. Oh yeah, there is no Hebrews 14. That is because such people don't make it into the record of Biblical heroes. When they had the opportunity to be refined in the fire, they chose to have fellowship with darkness and died full of bitterness, doubt, and unbelief. They chose to magnify the word of fear rather than the word of faith, and in having such fellowship with darkness they became like it. We become what we look at. Let us look to Jesus!

All of this is a picture of submitting to the Lamb on the throne. When we submit to the lamb on the throne, a river of living water will flow through us to the nations. I'm sure that because Stephen kept his eyes on Jesus, he began to change the situation that he was in to bring it into the obedience of Christ. That is actually the best context for baby Christians to be in: to have witnesses of Jesus in the flesh who show forth the praises of the one who called them from darkness into the light. It helps them to grow because fellowship with such people is actually having fellowship God! Such fellowship is a kingdom outpost. Such churches are the light of the world.

This is God's strategy for healing the nations, to thrust out laborers into the harvest which is all the world. It is absolutely beautiful. God desires that agape love should rule over all the earth. That includes every family, business, government and every sphere of life in the world. God's strategy is to send His sons who represent Him in the flesh. Robert Mearns likes to say, "Every problem in the world can be traced back to one thing: man rejected the government of God. The good news is that God will take them back again, but rebels don't get in." This saying is absolutely true, and every problem includes every socio-economic problem in the world. Everything that is wrong with the world, bar none, can be traced back to sin. The good news is that all sin has been dealt with at the cross. There is a river of life that flows from the savior's side that will bring healing to the nations. There is a river flowing from the temple of God, which will bring healing to the nations. God is sowing His sons into the world to bring it into the obedience of love, but it only works if they walk in love.

There is a very important awakening that is happening right now, and it has its influence in all kinds of Christian circles. It is an awareness that there is no secular and sacred divide. The only divide is clean and unclean. This is biblical, but unfortunately many in the Christian world have gotten away from such an awareness. We have held an unfortunate view of the separation of church and state that we have failed to see that the earth is the Lord's and that He shall reign over it all. He wants us to go into business, education, politics, arts and every sphere of life and bring it into the obedience of Christ. Sounds brutal until you realize it simply means that they will cause it to be a manifestation of love. They will cause all the nations of the earth to be blessed.

When I first started seeing this in scriptures, I preached a sermon on it and spent considerable time afterwards trying to convince people who were quite offended. They were offended at the possibility that God wanted more from them than a silent moral testimony in their workplace. They didn't want to see the responsibility God has given his people for the world. In truth, God wants His government of love to reign over every area of life.

Later that year I remember talking with Robert Mearns about the kingdom message at a King's Way Connection conference in Hungary. He was excited about what God was doing and was teaching everywhere that the great commission to go into all the world is a commission to go into *every* world, whether it is the world of business, politics, education or any sphere of life where people are involved, and to bring those places into the order of heaven. Jesus gave His life for the world. Such a message is life giving and it also activates many people into ministry in ways that they will not complain about because they are doing what God really created them to do in the first place. We can make disciples while making music, working in business, government, education, technology or any other arena of life. Not only that, but the market place knows what it is worth and pays for it. There is provision for the ministry in the ministry itself. Such teaching gives the right dignity to every part of the body of Christ and gets them involved in being a blessing. It activates them in a ministry that is far more beautiful than trying to trick people to church. It is absolutely beautiful.

The concept actually makes a lot of sense if people were to think about it. When someone comes to Christ do you think that Jesus wants to be lord of all their life? Do you think that this will change the way we interact in families? Then do you think God wants to be Lord of families? How about when we go to work? Do you think he wants to be our Lord there? Absolutely! Will that change how business is done? The bottom line is that obedience to the Lordship of Jesus will radically transform every level of society. It is absolutely wonderful.

There is one job that God gave Adam and Eve that I bet they didn't complain about. It was the job of populating the earth. In those days there was no pain involved in it. It is quite different now. The great commission is basically a mandate to populate the planet with children of God. This will actually extend the realm on the earth where love reigns. What a glorious job! I am willing to bet that when you are doing the job God created you to do, you will actually be satisfied and full of thanks and praise.

If you are given a job, then there should be a strategy. I think the strategy is that people need to see Jesus. Many people seem to think that for a person to come to Christ they need to "hit rock bottom." If we limit our thinking to such a thing, then we should be praying curses down upon all the earth because we need it to get bad enough for people to receive Jesus so they can go to heaven when they die. No wonder Christians are often accused of being escapists.

It is true that often times God has to break up the fallow ground. It is true that in His mercy He will show his wrath on sin. It is also true that unless sin is dealt with, it will cause incredible suffering and death. It is true that this is often a place where people turn to the Lord. Yet this must not be the primary model upon which we build, there is another model that is absolutely beautiful. I believe God's preferred way is the way of the Queen of Sheba. Testimony of the glory of Solomon's kingdom brought her to see for herself, and in seeing she was convinced. Hallelujah!

Scripture calls us to pray for the peace of wherever we live (e.g. 2 Tim 2:1-4). We are called to pray for those who are in authority because God wants everyone to be blessed. Even more, such peace creates a context that makes faith natural. The gospel calls us to interact with the world through love whether it is as a parent, spouse, worker, governor, or any other role that we play. When people see the kingdom of love, it will make it natural for them to believe in Jesus. Look at the primary strategy of Jesus. He healed the sick, which revealed the love of God. He cast out devils which revealed the love of God. He fed the hungry, loved the outcast, and defended the poor and weak. He forgave people and in every way he manifested who God is. He certainly did drive out the money changers, and he was not always gentle Jesus, meek and mild. You could find him rebuking Peter as Satan and proclaiming harsh words of Judgment, but it was always towards the proud. He always showed grace toward the humble. All of this is a manifestation of the appropriate actions of love. Everything He did manifested the love of God in the flesh. This manifestation of the love of God is the way the first generation church operated. It is the way we are going to operate.

This is also why so much of the New Testament is training on how to live this out in daily life in every situation of life. For example, if a child grows up in a home and sees his/her father and mother love each other, it makes believing in a loving, heavenly father no major leap of faith. When children grow up in broken homes where they are abused and the parents do not exhibit love, it becomes a tough leap of faith to believe in a loving heavenly father. Especially if the parents are professing Christians. Gloriously, God rescues such people all the time, but they often find it very hard to give up control over their lives. They try to control things because of fear. It makes trusting God difficult and trusting self a natural safety net. Such trust in self God often has to remove.

The same thing is true in every area of life. If we see the government of Jesus manifested in the flesh it becomes very easy to believe that Jesus has power to save. We cannot deny the great signs and wonders that are before our eyes. In truth, a home, business, church, or anywhere that love reigns is just as much a miracle as a dead person being raised back to life. A person being free from fear and walking in love is the greatest testimony and witness to the power of Jesus Christ.

God wants to send kingdom ambassadors into every arena of life and have them bring it into the obedience of Christ, or in other words, have them governed by love. The implications are tremendous. Think about people who actually are a blessing to others no matter who they are. They do not just want to be a blessing, but they actually are a blessing because they have received power from on high to walk in love. God wants everyone to experience His love and His ways whether they are Christians or not. He causes it to rain on the righteous and unrighteous alike. He would have all people experience the love, mercy, grace, forgiveness, and life that is in Christ, and He would like them to experience it from His representatives on the earth. That is His kingdom strategy.

I remember when I was with a pastor in Nigeria and he told me about how corrupt the police force is. He told me that all the churches teach that Christians cannot become police officers because it would corrupt them. I told him that it was very unfortunate that the churches were teaching such things because it in essence keeps that part of the world under the dominion of darkness. The very thing that is needed is that Christians get in there and bring it under the obedience of love. The church needs to sow men and women into every area of the world who have a good reputation, wisdom, and the Holy Spirit. Why? Because they must have the power to walk in love when all the pressures of the world are telling them to compromise. They must be witnesses who would die before they would deny the Lord. Such people will overcome the enemy and bring the nations into the obedience of Christ.

Think about the beauty of a home where Jesus is manifested as Lord. Think about the love, the grace, the hope, the unity and all of the blessings of the presence of God. It would be a blessing for a child to grow up in such a home. The church is meant to be an institution that empowers kingdom homes. Think about having to go to work where there is unity, respect, love, hope, peace and the kingdom of God. It would be a wonderful blessing for anyone to work in such a place. The church is meant to be an institution that empowers such kingdom businesses. What if the industry was the music or movie industry? What if all people involved in that industry used their talents for the common blessing of all rather than exploiting people to make a buck. I think such an industry would be an incredible blessing to any people. What if it was the food industry and they provided the healthiest food for the least amount of money. What if they took the health and wealth of the nation to be their primary concern rather than their investors or if that was their investor's primary purpose? I think they would be an incredible blessing. Think about a government where all the elected officials had wisdom from God, didn't accept bribes, did what was right no matter the personal cost, and made the government to be a blessing to everyone. Such a nation would surely be a wonderful place to live. May God thrust out laborers into the field of the world.

I would even suggest that if every institution in a nation was coming into the obedience of Christ, such a nation would have quite a manifestation of the presence of God. So much so it may even be undeniable. I think that such nations may even be able to provoke Israel to jealousy.

What if people actually measured their success in how much of a blessing they could be to others? Such a simple definition of success, if lived out, would have tremendous socio-economic implications. It would certainly bless somebody. Yet there is the whole issue of bondage to sin. We can work out intellectually the incredible blessing it would be if people would live according to the law, yet we find that people act contrary to what they morally admire when put in pressing situations. The fire will reveal all things. They end up doing the very thing that they hate. As long as this is the case, then it is impossible that there should ever be a manifestation of heavenly government upon the earth. But if the gospel of Jesus Christ actually empowers people to walk in love rather than simply commanding them to do so, then there is incredible hope that the nations could be brought into the obedience of Christ, but only once our obedience is first fulfilled.

If it is true that Jesus can actually deliver us from the law of sin and death and empower us to walk in love, then there are incredible possibilities and incredible grounds for hope. I would proclaim that in the Gospel this is exactly what God has done through Jesus Christ crucified.

Spiritual DNA

—◊◊◊—

We see that when we were born again we became Children of God. We actually have His life in us, but we are born spiritual babies. Though we are literally children of God, we appear as children of the world until we come of age. What we mean is that even though we are legitimately children of God, as long as we walk in the flesh, we will stink with sin. If put in the right context and fed the right spiritual food, we will grow up. If put in the wrong context and fed the wrong food, we will never grow up. We need to structure church so that people grow up in Christ.

God has a strategy to get people to grow, and it is through the anointing and gifts of the Spirit. We must be filled with the Holy Spirit. He actually has a ministry for every child of God, even in their immaturity, that will actually play a role in bringing people into spiritual maturity. When every member does their part, it will cause growth. The reason why this is so important is that we become like him as we see him. Through the anointing of the Spirit we can see the Lord in the most immature baby. Through this empowering of the Spirit people will rise up in the most unusual situations and give witness to Jesus!

The other side is that while people are still growing up spiritually, we must cover their faults with love. As long as people still have a heart to grow up in Christ, then we must never give up on them. We must love them into life. We have a responsibility to do so. We must forgive, encourage, rebuke, pray and do anything God calls us to do to help carry their burdens. In our need they will do the same for us. This is how the church works.

Growing up in Christ can actually be very beautiful in a good home. We actually experience His presence His love, and His word that gives life. We experience mercy, grace, forgiveness, peace, joy and everything that has to do with the kingdom of God. We receive encouragement when we are going through the trials and embracing the cross. We receive the counsel of wisdom when we are faced with tough situations. We learn to grow up into the image of Christ. This learning takes place in the context of daily life. It happens as we are husbands, wives, fathers, mothers and children. It happens as we interact with the world in love at school, at work, at play. As we grow in Christ, the revelation of the kingdom begins to influence every sphere of life in increasing measure. As we are faithful with little, much more becomes entrusted to us. We find that He will satisfy our heart's desire to be a blessing by giving us the power to be a blessing.

The goal of the church is to work to bring the government of God in the earth. This is done by sending the sons of God into all the world. How does this happen? We see people born again by the word of God, filled with the Holy Spirit and grow into spiritual maturity and they will by nature extend the government of God wherever they are.

Not only is the church called to raise up sons for God, but the church itself is coming to maturity. The ministry of the Apostles, prophets, evangelists, pastors and teachers are in operation until we all come to a perfect man, to the measure of the stature of the fullness of Christ. Jesus is at work in His church to cleanse her so that she will be without spot or wrinkle or any such thing. He will make her holy and without blemish just as He is. She will be a glorious church. This is what God is doing.

> "So it was, when the people set out from their camp to cross over the Jordan, with the priests bearing the ark of the covenant before the people, and as those who bore the ark came to the Jordan, and the feet of the priests who bore the ark dipped in the edge of the water (for the Jordan overflows all its banks during the whole time of harvest), that the waters which came down from upstream stood still, and rose in a heap very far away at Adam, the city that is beside Zaretan. So the waters that went down into the Sea of the Arabah, the Salt Sea, failed, and were cut off; and the

people crossed over opposite Jericho." (Jos 3:14-16 NKJV)

Notice that when Israel crossed over into the Promised Land, the river Jordan was stopped from Adam to the Dead Sea. This is prophetic of the church coming to maturity. We crossed over the Red Sea into the wilderness as a spiritual babe. The church will cross over the Jordan and come into her inheritance. She will walk in the government of God. She will be mature. The curse that flowed from Adam's sin into death will be destroyed. The way this will happen is when spiritual babes in Christ grow up. Just like Moses went through the wilderness and came forth first, so shall there be a people who come to maturity before others in order to serve others. The same pattern is all through scripture and it is no wonder that we see the same thing in Jesus who gave birth to the church in the first place. He was manifested to destroy the works of the devil and now He is doing it by raising up sons for God. He is very good at it too.

"For the earnest expectation of the creation eagerly waits for the revealing of the sons of God. For the creation was subjected to futility, not willingly, but because of Him who subjected it in hope; because the creation itself also will be delivered from the bondage of corruption into the glorious liberty of the children of God." (Ro 8:19-21 NKJV)

As the sons of God come to maturity it will have revolutionary impact on the world. It was all in the DNA we received when we were born again but it needs to come to maturity for it to be manifested. How will we get there? Will it be by works of the law or by the hearing of faith? How will we grow up into Christ? As we see Him we will be like him. As we receive the gift of God that is in one another and freely give the gift that God has entrusted to us, we will all grow up into Him who is the head. He is coming back for a pure spotless bride, a glorious church!

Printed in the United States
209437BV00001B/112-315/P

9 781607 911913